Ingrid

My Swedish-American Life and Adventures

D1570993

INGRID BERGSTROM

Ingrid

MY SWEDISH-AMERICAN LIFE AND ADVENTURES

Swedish-American Historical Society
Chicago, Illinois

ISBN 0-914819-03-8

Dedicated with love
to my husband Gösta

And in memory of my mother and father
and my brother Erik

FOREWORD

IT IS WITH IMMENSE PLEASURE that the Swedish-American Historical Society is publishing the memoirs of one of its long-time members and friends, Ingrid Bergstrom. This is an important and interesting book for several reasons, not least because of its author. The adventures of Ingrid and her husband Gösta help tell the story of what life has been like for Swedish immigrants of a later era (post-World War II), which has both contrast and continuity with the period of mass migration prior to 1930, to which most Swedish Americans trace their ancestry. Moreover, this is an important chapter of women's history, as well as a slice of Chicago history. In these ways, the experiences of Ingrid and Gösta in America, with ongoing ties to the homeland, have many typical characteristics. Yet, the life of this most remarkable woman is hardly ordinary. Ingrid's life has been singular from the beginning, and her way of recounting it is lively and engaging, a mirror of herself. This book will attract readers for many reasons. Richly illustrated, we join her in her journey of life and love.

Several of Ingrid's friends have contributed to its compilation, and many more have waited expectantly for its appearance. Risé Sanders-Wier, a documentary filmmaker and freelance writer, first met Ingrid while producing a documentary on the Swedish community in Chicago for WTTW/PBS television. A very successful production, Ingrid's appearance and stories led Risé to be a catalyst for preparing the book that so many others had encouraged her to write, including a hand in compiling the recipe section. The primary motivator, Shirley Öst Johnson of Portland, Oregon (who had worked for Ingrid at the Sweden

Shop while a student at North Park College), was truly instrumental in working with Ingrid to take her notes and recorded stories and generate a structured narrative, a true labor of love. Shirley's daughter, Greta Elisabeth Lann, a gifted artist living in Stockholm, Sweden, produced the art for the cover and the chapter headings.

The copy-editing of Eloise Nelson has been, in her customary manner, meticulous and sensitive. She has worked closely with Ingrid and the Society in many of the details necessary to the book's production. Sonja Nelson, office manager of the Swedish-American Historical Society, formatted and laid out the copy, along with the professional expertise of David Westerfield, who did so much to shepherd the book to press. Finally, Dag Blanck has lent his scholarly eye to the project, and has written an introduction placing the narrative in its larger historical context. Thank you to all.

Acknowledgements duly made, this is Ingrid's book, and all who know her and Gösta hear their voices quite distinctly, caught up in the ongoing journey of this unique couple. We are grateful, Ingrid, that you have shared your life together with us, and we look forward to learning of its future chapters.

Philip J. Anderson
President, Swedish-American Historical Society
Chair, Publications Committee

INTRODUCTION

SWEDISH EMIGRATION to the United States did not come to a halt at the end of the 1920s. To be sure, that decade witnessed the cessation of what is usually called the era of Swedish mass migration to the United States, when some 1.3 million Swedes arrived between 1840 and 1930. The Great Depression and World War II meant that the rate of migration between 1930 and 1945 was very small, and, in fact, the majority of Swedes moving between Sweden and the U.S. during that time were immigrants returning to Sweden.

Following the end of World War II, however, the borders that had been closed during the war were re-opened, and traveling back and forth between the countries became possible once again. Ties between Sweden and Swedish America were re-established, and 1946 became the first time in many years that Swedish Americans in substantial numbers were once again able to visit the "old country."[1] It is also interesting to note that during these years many Swedes argued that it was time for Sweden to pay greater attention to its descendants on the other side of the Atlantic, as well as make sure that they felt welcome on their "return" journeys to Sweden.[2]

The migration flow also went the other direction, and for the first time in some two decades, Swedes once again began emigrating to America. As historian H. Arnold Barton has pointed out, it is difficult more precisely to ascertain the size of the post-

---

[1] Cf. H. Arnold Barton, "The Summer of '46," *Swedish-American Historical Quarterly*, 35 (January 1984), 3-5.

[2] Anna-Lenah Elgström, "Review of Adolph Benson, *Sweden & The American Revolution*," *Svenska Dagbladet*, 24 June 1946; "Attityden till Svensk-Amerika," *Dagens Nyheter*, 9 August, 1946.

World War II migration, but he estimates that between 1945 and the present time, around 60,000 Swedes have emigrated to the United States, five percent of the total number of immigrants during the era of mass immigration.[3] From an American point of view, these modern immigrants constitute a much smaller part of the American ethnic and immigrant mosaic than did their predecessors in the nineteenth and early twentieth centuries. Modern Swedish immigrants are but a trickle when compared to other immigrant groups in the U.S. today.

This group of immigrants differs significantly from its compatriots of the earlier period. Economic hardship, the basic reason for the Swedish mass immigration, is no longer the major impetus for Swedish migration to North America. Since the close of the mass immigration period in the late 1920s, Sweden has undergone a major transformation process, becoming a prosperous and modern European country, and at times has even been admired as a source of inspiration for other countries.[4]

The reasons for Swedish emigration to the U.S. in modern times are varied, and, to many, the opportunities for professional and educational advancement have been important. Many Swedish corporations have a presence in the United States, and American companies of different kinds have attracted many Swedes as a place of employment for longer or shorter periods of time. In addition, Swedish students have chosen to study in exchange programs and foreign universities in large numbers during the past few decades. In 2002, for example, it was estimated that over 4,500 Swedes were enrolled as undergraduates in

[3] H. Arnold Barton, "The Latest Wave. Swedish Immigrants to the United States Since World War II," in Lars Olsson & Sune Åkerman, eds., *Hembygden & Världen. Festskrift till Ulf Beijbom* (Växjö, 2002), 106.

[4] The American journalist Marquis Child coined the phrase "the middle way" in his highly complimentary book *Sweden—The Middle Way* (New Haven, Conn., 1936), and the American political scientist Steven Kelman has observed "that Sweden has received an attention from scholars and from those interested in social policy far disproportionate to its population of 8 million and its peripheral status in world affairs." (Quoted after John Louge, "The Swedish Model: Visions of Sweden in American Politics and Political Science," Swedish-American Historical Quarterly, 50 [July 1999], p. 162. The Swedish "model" has also been criticized, at times severely. See, for example, Ronald Huntford, *The New Totalitarians* [London, 1971]).

American colleges or universities, placing Sweden fourth among Western European countries sending students to the United States, after Germany, the United Kingdom, and France.[5]

The many strong links, and what can be called a "migration tradition" that exist between Sweden and the United States as a result of the mass immigration between 1840 and 1930, is another factor that can explain the continued Swedish migration to the U.S. The awareness of America in Sweden continues to be very strong, and many Swedes continue to have American relatives and friends, making the U.S. a leading migration destination. Yet another reason is the feeling of isolation that has existed in Sweden, in particular during the years after the end of World War II, when travel outside the country had been virtually impossible for almost six years.

One striking aspect of Swedish emigration to the U.S. after 1945 is its feminine character. A distinctly larger number of Swedish women than men have emigrated, and today the American Census Bureau records that 60 percent of the Swedish-born residents in America are women, a higher proportion than ever before. This number most likely reflects the not insignificant number of Swedish women who through education or work have met and married an American and have subsequently settled in his homeland, pointing to love as yet another modern reason for immigration.

Ingrid Bergstrom's book about her life as a modern Swedish immigrant in America provides us with a vivid illustration of some of these characteristics. She writes about her eagerness to live in another country, and of the excitement that America provided to a young Swedish couple in the late 1940s. Once in America, Ingrid continues to work at restaurants—just as she had done in Sweden. Her lively story illustrates an immigrant's encounter with America, and tells of the search for work and housing. Ingrid and Gösta are quite successful in America, eventually establishing themselves as business owners, and when

5 *Chronicle of Higher Education,* 22 November, 2002.

Gösta turns 50, able to travel around the world to celebrate his birthday. The relative ease with which modern immigrants can travel across the Atlantic is also evident, as they go back to Sweden many times, and eventually even buy a summer home in Ingrid's old home province of Dalarna.

The Swedish-American community has played an important role in the life of the Bergstroms. As a recent immigrant in New York, Ingrid found her first job at the Swedish-American restaurant Three Crowns, eventually continuing work at Bit of Sweden in Hollywood and at the Kungsholm in Chicago. Once they had settled in Chicago, the old capital of Swedish America, Ingrid and Gösta also became heavily involved in its lively and varied Swedish-American organizational life, founding one group (Svenska gillet) and eventually taking over the Swedish-American "landmark," the Verdandi Club on North Clark Street, where Sven Jerring was one of the many prominent Swedish visitors, and where one of the selections on the jukebox was "Hälsa dem där hemma."

To move from one country to another is, perhaps, an experience that causes a person to reflect on her life from a particular perspective, and sometimes compels her to share it with others. Ingrid Bergstrom has clearly led a full and interesting life, bridging Sweden and America, and her story should remind us of the many common threads and increase our understanding of the lives of all immigrants, Swedish or non-Swedish.

Dag Blanck
Centre for Multiethnic Studies, Uppsala University, Sweden
Director, Swenson Swedish Immigration Research Center, Augustana
*   College, Rock Island, Illinois*

AUTHOR'S PREFACE

As I GOT OLDER and things slowed down for us, I was looking for something to do. I wasn't looking too hard though. I had some friends who kept saying that I should write a book. They said that anyone who had been around like we had might have some stories to tell. I didn't think they were serious at first, but after awhile I started to think back and remember many funny and interesting things that did happen.

I got really excited and started writing. I soon found myself living in the past, and that was so enjoyable too. So I kept writing, sometimes in the middle of the night, and in Swedish, of course. I couldn't do this in English or it would be in Swinglish, as people say. I knew I would need some help in getting it down on paper.

I heard from a friend of ours who had worked for us years ago, and her letters and her account of her trip to Sweden were so entertaining. I read them over and over again, and I thought of her when it came time to get serious. I contacted Shirley Öst Johnson, and she agreed to help and even came to our house for a few days to hear some of the stories herself. She has a family and lives in Oregon. She went home and waited for my tapes to arrive. Her daughter Greta Lann developed beautiful artwork.

In the meantime, I started thinking about the book, and I couldn't stop talking about it when I was with people. I wondered what they were thinking. Did they think I was presumptuous? Oh, well, I was having fun, and who knows where this will go?

Then Queen Sylvia of Sweden came to Chicago for a reception at the Swedish American Museum Center, and I had the chance to meet her. I have written about this in Chapter 36 of the book, how she said she wants to read my book. Well, then, I thought, maybe others will want to read it, too. So now I have to write the book!

I want to thank Kerstin Lane, executive director of the Swedish American Museum Center, for her encouragement. Without it, this book would never have been written. Many talented people have become involved in helping with this book, as Philip Anderson mentions in his Foreword. I want to thank all of them, my husband Gösta for his patience, as well as all of the friends who have helped me to have the life I have lived.

Ingrid Bergstrom
Chicago, Illinois

CONTENTS

My dad was always riding his bike around the village, up until the age of 99.

Our family in 1923—my father Martin, me at age 2, Signe at age 5, and our mother Matilda, who was expecting Erik at the time.

My brother Erik was two years younger than I. He didn't like watching my plays, but we were always close friends. He died in 2002.

Growing Up
in Dalarna

MY STORY begins on the top deck of the *Gripsholm*, one of two ships that left Göteborg (Gothenburg), Sweden, each week in the 1940s for the United States. It was 1947. I had been sea-sick for days. And so discouraged. What was it like where we were going, and what were we leaving behind? I sat in a deck chair, all bundled up, with the waves splashing up on the ship. Every once in awhile I felt the mist on my face. That seemed to help me in my thoughts, and I began to feel better.

I was thinking back—way back to my childhood. I was born Ingrid Elisabeth to Martin and Matilda Westerholm on January 15, 1921, in Dala-Husby, Dalarna, Sweden. The province of Dalarna is in the heart of Sweden, where the old folk customs are still carried on and the people speak a regional dialect.

I have memories of wanting to be an actress, or a Sunday school teacher, from when I was about six or seven years old. I had a sister, Signe, three years older, but I only told my brother, Erik, two years younger, of my ambitions. He was my audience when I performed, and I made him sit still and watch and even applaud! He hated that and reminded me about it for many years afterward. My mother knew, too, because she would hang a white cloth in the doorway for a curtain so I would have a stage. I would come from behind the curtain and suddenly appear,

Our family cafe was a popular place for travelers passing through Dala-Husby. Our church (at right) is one of the oldest churches in Sweden.

ready to act out whatever was running through my imagination.

Our family had a business on the main highway in town near the bridge that crosses the river Dalälven and near our beautiful old church. The church has been standing there since the 1200s. We owned a gasoline station (Standard Oil) and a cafe where we sold sandwiches and coffee. In the summertime, we would set up tables outside and serve our customers in the garden. It was lovely.

Coming from Stockholm, the tourists had to drive past our cafe and gas station on their way to the popular vacation areas of Rättvik and Mora on Lake Siljan. If they needed gas, I would fill their tank for them even when I was only nine or ten years old. Our pump held twenty-five liters. If they wanted thirty liters, I gave them twenty-five and then would pump the tank to fill it up so I could give them their last five liters. My right arm got very strong.

My mother had dark blonde hair, and was very kind and mild-mannered. Although we didn't have much, she had a way of making us feel that we had everything. My father had dark hair and eyes. He was strong-willed and less patient. He had a good business head, and both parents had great energy and worked very hard. I can see myself in both of them.

Our father thought we should work hard, too, so once we were home from school our work began. Maybe it was good for us. We were healthy kids, almost never sick, and we certainly learned how to work.

We lived in a large white house, a former dairy, a four- or five-minute walk from our cafe. We had a big vegetable garden, all kinds of flowers, and raspberries that grew large and sweet on the long summer days. My mother loved gardening, but with our busy cafe she never had much time for that. Dad enjoyed taking care of a neighbor's horses, and he liked to go fishing now and then.

We started school when we were seven. I liked school, and we had good teachers. Each day began with a hymn, and then we had twenty minutes of religious instruction. We learned a lot of

Our home in Dala-Husby was formerly a dairy farm. We had a beautiful view of the Dalälven River.

psalms and hymns by heart. That was good for us.

When I was in third grade, a new music teacher came to our school. The first thing he did was teach us how to sing, and he gave us small mirrors so we could check our mouths when we sang. He also led the music at our church. We had very good choirs. Every Christmas morning he would sing "Ave Maria" from the church balcony, where the organ was located, and it was so beautiful. He was a well-loved man. To this day, children still get good music training in the schools in Sweden.

Every child got a little metal bank in school, and once a month the bank came and emptied them and wrote down the amount we saved. But I wanted to go to the bank myself, so every two or three days I'd run over there and deposit ten or fifteen *öre* (half a cent or less). I felt special doing that. My

My bank book. The bank said that 2 *öre* saved every day would grow to 226 *kronor* in twenty years. By that time I was 27 years old and living in America.

mother sometimes gave me twenty-five or fifty *öre* to deposit so I wouldn't run to the bank so often. I learned that it's good to start early to get the habit of saving because you never know what tomorrow will bring.

When we weren't in school or working, we kids had fun playing ball. We learned to ride bikes when we were five or six years old. I liked to ride as fast as possible. In the winter we would ice skate on the river or go skiing, and I loved going around in the snow on a *spark*, a kind of stand-up sled.

At Christmastime, we would get one or two presents, none of which cost any money. When I was seven or eight years old, my dad gave me a little bell from one of the horses he took care of. I still have it and cherish it to this day.

My brother and I also helped on a farm in the area. At the *herrgård* (manor house estate), we picked *rovor* (turnips), row by row. They would be stored and later used as food for the cows. It was hard work. If the day was hot and sunny, we would take a break and jump in the river and swim. At that time, logs were floated to the mill on the river, and it was great fun to disappear under the logs and then come up and float on them.

My mother was very religious and was from one of the free churches. My father was not religious, but he was concerned that we go to Sunday school. On Sundays, we would go to the Lutheran church in the morning and to the Baptist chapel at 2:00 in the afternoon. I was confirmed in the Lutheran church.

I had a little friend who often warned me about hell. One reason I wanted to be a Sunday school teacher was because I thought if I became a Sunday school teacher then I would certainly go to heaven. One afternoon I was crying and crying because my friend said the world was soon coming to an end. My mother was so comforting and tried to calm my fears.

When I was sixteen, my sister Signe was running the cafe. She had taken it over when she was nineteen. I would help by serving coffee and drinks. Although we had a refrigerator at the time, we kept the drinks in the basement where it was cold, so I did a lot of running up and down the stairs.

One summer we met some tourists who were staying at the inn in our village. They owned a restaurant in Stockholm. They came over and had coffee with us and liked our pastries, tortes, and sandwiches better than the inn's. One day they asked my sister if she would make a home-cooked meal for them. She said no, she couldn't do that (after all, they were from Stockholm and probably quite fussy). I asked her if I could. She said okay, but she ended up making the food anyway, and I cheerfully served it to them.

At the end of their vacation, when they were getting ready to leave, the couple asked if I would come and work for them in their restaurant. I was seventeen and had completed regular school. I really wanted to do this and asked my parents to allow me to go. Since my grandmother lived in Stockholm and I would have a job, they said yes. So off I went to start my new life in the big city.

As I sat on the deck of the *Gripsholm*, I realized that this decision was the turning point and beginning of a journey that would take me to America.

Meeting
Someone Special

I WORKED for the owners of the Social Institute Restaurant in Stockholm for two years, and those were good years. I also lived with them, and they paid me well. This restaurant served the Social Institute and the nearby university.

It was a high-class restaurant, with an excellent menu of sandwiches, fish, meat, and potatoes. Our waitress uniforms were pretty, with green and gray stripes on the skirt, a green top, and a green stripe on the apron edge. We worked every day from 11:00 a.m. to 8:00 p.m. The restaurant was closed on Sundays and holidays.

I remember that the owners at first had to tell me to keep my voice down. When I was ordering the food, my country dialect carried all the way into the dining room. I took the hint, and after that the chef could barely hear me.

The restaurant was located on Odengatan near Stockholm University. I still remember some of the professors who came in. A few became well-known in Sweden, and I would read their names in the paper sometimes—Karin Kock, Nanna Schwartz, and Herbert Tingsten.

On my Sundays off, my friends and I would go to Skansen, Grönalund amusement park, and to a little restaurant called Prague, where we ordered tea and toast, the cheapest thing on the menu. I was enjoying life in the big city.

After working at the restaurant for about two years, I got sick with rheumatic fever and had to go home to recuperate. I took medicine baths and was wrapped in something called "fat cotton." My father didn't think that was doing any good, so he took me to a homeopath doctor who gave me some pills, and I got better in no time.

Then I was ready to return to Stockholm. It was 1940 and not an easy time to get a job. I went to live with my grandmother in her apartment at Norrtullsgatan 20 in the city. After trying unsuccessfully for a couple of weeks to find a job, I was discouraged enough that I wanted to go home.

My grandmother said, "Stay one day more, because I think there will be something in the paper tomorrow that will make you very happy. You just stay; you will get coffee and apple turnovers in bed, and you can read the paper." I knew she wanted me to remain with her in Stockholm, so I decided to try once more to find a job.

That was when I found that *one little ad*. I told her, "There is one ad for a waitress here, and I can at least go and see where it is." When I walked into the restaurant, there were eighteen girls looking for work. I decided I didn't care if I got the job or not because the cafe wasn't as attractive as the place I had worked before. Either I would stay and take the job if offered, or I would go home and work for my sister.

I took my time going back to my grandmother's, and when I walked into the apartment she said, "I have ironed a dress for you. You are supposed to start work at 4:00 o'clock today!"

I started work at 4:00, and at 6:00 or 7:00 o'clock that evening I met my future husband! He came in with four other guys, and I still remember that they ordered hot chocolate and sandwiches. They sat together at their table and laughed a lot. Later on, I heard that Gösta Bergström had said, "That is the girl I'm going to marry."

For the next two weeks, Gösta would come in every morning before work and order a cup of coffee and two sweet rolls. He paid two *kronor*, the equivalent of fifty-two cents, thirty-eight cents for the food and fourteen cents for the tip. I thought he was so handsome with his blue-black hair, and he had the most beautiful hands. I knew what time he came in, so I would play romantic Hawaiian music on the record player, and we would enjoy a little conversation.

After two weeks of this, he asked me to go to a movie with him. From then on we were a pair. We spent a lot of time together going to movies, riding bikes, taking walks, and going to a *konditori* (coffee shop) where they had live music. Being with him seemed so natural. He was such a good man, and I liked everything about him. He sometimes said that he was a little too shy, but that was probably good because I talk too much. He said he liked that about me, that I was so full of life.

This was February, and we became engaged on Midsummer Eve, a special holiday in late June that celebrates the longest day of the year. We were married on *Annandagjul*, the day after Christmas, in 1941 in the Kungsholm Church in Stockholm. It

We were married the day after Christmas in 1941. I was twenty years old.

was a small wedding with thirty to forty people and my family from Dalarna. We rented a small apartment near the center of town and furnished it with what we could afford.

A couple of years ago, we celebrated our sixtieth wedding anniversary. Our friends had a big party for us, and Gösta gave a little speech. He said, "I came from Lycksele, Lappland, and was very shy and bashful. Then I met Ingrid from Dalarna, and she was full of life, laughing and talking, and it was love at first sight. They used to say, *'Lika barn leka bäst,'* which means 'The same play best together,' but we have to change that because we are so different and we've had such a wonderful life!" It was so kind what he said.

My grandmother had been right in telling me to stay another day. I might never have met Gösta otherwise.

Gösta grew up on this farm in Lycksele, Lappland. His house is on the left.

Our Stockholm Cafe

OH, THE MEMORIES are coming so fast! The weather is bad, and it's stirring up the ocean and me at the same time. What are we doing, being on this ship? I need to think about Sweden and my family so I don't forget. I must never forget.

After Gösta and I had been married for awhile, we thought we might be interested in buying a cafe. We mentioned this to the owner of the cafe where I worked, and he said, "Why don't you buy this one? We want to sell it and open another one, one with a Hawaiian theme here in Stockholm." At that time,

Our cafe in Stockholm, where we sold a lot of coffee.

Gösta on an auditing assignment in Avesta, Sweden. Business at our cafe was so good that he finally had to quit his accounting job.

Hawaiian food and music were popular in Sweden. It was 1942, the war was on, and people weren't traveling because of the war, so anything Hawaiian seemed very exotic.

So we bought Kaffestugan. It was a good business even though it wasn't fancy. Just some tables and chairs, flowers here and there, good coffee and coffee bread, and tasty sandwiches.

It was located near our apartment, and there was good parking on the side streets. We catered to the working class and to men who were delivery drivers. We also had delivery boys on bikes, the kind that had the name of the business on them. Since we were on a side street, no one would see that they had taken a bit of time off. We played American music on our jukebox, and they would come in just to listen to that. Full house we had all the time.

It was a lot of work. We opened at 6:00 a.m. and closed at 10:00 p.m. every day of the week, except on Sunday we could be a bit lazy and open at 10:00 a.m. and close at 8:00 p.m. I was twenty-one years old and full of energy.

I needed to be since Gösta had kept his accounting job at Bohlin's accounting firm, auditing restaurants and factories. His office was on Stureplan, one of the main thoroughfares. Bohlin's is a large firm, still in business today. Gösta had studied accounting in Sundsvall, then came to Stockholm and found work. He has always been fantastic with figures and at managing money.

I was the one who opened the cafe and served coffee to the early customers. Every morning at about 7:00, I would say to them, "Watch the door. I'll be right back with some fresh cinnamon and cardamom rolls." I would run to the bakery down the street and pick up a huge tray of freshly baked sweet rolls, about fifty of them. As I walked back with the rolls, they smelled so good. The customers would hold open the door and be waiting for me and for fresh cinnamon rolls. We were always very busy at that time of day.

We also ran a contest with the waitresses to see how many cups of coffee they could sell each day. This gave us some control since we didn't have a cash register, just a box we put the money in. They would count the coffee cups they took to the dishwasher, and I would keep track of them. About 250 cups a day was the average, and we had only twenty-eight chairs in the cafe.

Since we kept an account for each girl, she would go to a customer who had ordered milk and a sandwich and say, "Aren't you

Our customers would be waiting for freshly baked cinnamon rolls when I opened our cafe each morning. They smelled so good!

going to have a cup of coffee, too?" We sold so much coffee that I could afford to give a couple of little prizes to those who sold the most in a month.

The first-prize winner would receive twenty *kronor* (about $2.50 today), and the second-place winner would get a ticket to a movie. Since we had no more than three waitresses, they had a good chance of winning. The customers knew about the contest, too, and the girls enjoyed telling them when they had won. It was all so much fun, and because of that we sold a lot of coffee.

On December 13, Lucia Day, we treated everyone to coffee, *lussekatter* (Lucia saffron rolls), and a small glass of *glögg* (spiced wine). We did this all day long, and people appreciated it. People came from all over to our restaurant. Our business was so good that Gösta had to quit his job at Bohlin's and help out.

Trying Out
the Film Industry

GÖSTA'S FATHER was visiting Stockholm, and he could make all kinds of faces. Gösta said, "Papa is so funny, I think he could be in movies."

"I could, too," I said.

"Oh, no, what could you do?"

"All kinds of things."

"I don't believe you."

When he said that, I wanted to show him I could.

I found a little picture of me that I had taken at a dime store for twenty-five *öre* (a few cents). I sent it to the film studio and said I would like to be in the movies. Surprisingly, I got an answer right away. I should come to their address the following week and be dressed in a long evening gown. I was going to be in a scene in a fancy restaurant, in the year 1920.

Well, I had never had a long evening gown, and I didn't want to buy one, so I went to a shop on Drottningatan, the pedestrian street, and rented one. It was the most beautiful dress, with a white skirt, a shiny top, and a black overcoat.

I went there by taxi, fully dressed and feeling very special. When I got there, I realized the others had come on bicycles and changed clothes there. I came in style, I tell you. The first thing they did was change my pageboy hairdo and comb it in an upswept style. I liked that.

The scene went well, but I didn't know how to get them to call me back again. I could be a bit conniving at times, and I said, "Next time you call me, I'll bring some coffee beans." Coffee beans were hard to get. "Do you mean that?" the man in charge said. "We will have a big party then. But can you type?"

"No, I cannot type."

He needed someone for a scene of a young woman typing. "Well, then, I'll photograph you from the back, and we won't see your fingers."

I went in and out with my little bag of coffee beans several times. My husband thought they liked me for more than the coffee, and I think they did, too.

I had this photo taken in Stockholm around the time I was working in films.

We had a lot of coffee because the rationing was based on how much coffee we sold in our cafe. During that time, more than a hundred apartments were being built in our area. The construction workers would order coffee and sandwiches from us, and our *brickflicka* (girl with a tray) would take it to the site. We had the best coffee in town and lots of it.

One of the movies I was in was *Rid I Natt* (translated into English as *Ride This Night*), based on a Vilhelm Moberg book. It was early in the morning and we were supposed to run in a forest. They had sprayed so it looked foggy, and they put extra lengths on the dogs' tails so they looked like wolves. We had to jump up on a big stone and scream, *"Vargen kommer! Vargen kommer!"* (The wolves are coming!). We were afraid of those wolves and scrambled up on that stone, all of us.

I also did some commercials. One was for a beauty salon, and in another I was the daughter getting married and the family didn't know what to give me. The mother was crocheting, and I asked her how she did it. Then the father remembered the store, Tuppens Lakansväv, and their fancy sheets and linens. So that was what I was going to get.

Another commercial was for a company selling furniture you could put together yourself. I was a newlywed coming back from a honeymoon, and there were big boxes waiting for us. The ad showed us putting the furniture together, and it was so easy even I could do it!

I saw that commercial in Sweden a few years ago on a show about films from the 1940s, since the ad came on before the film. I was in more ads as well, and I took classes to help take away my Dalarna dialect. I worked with some others on a commercial that won fourth prize, and I was also chosen for two test pilots.

My film career ended shortly after that. When one of the directors suggested *a way* for me to have more opportunity, I chose to stay away. I realized my happy life with Gösta and our Kaffestugan were most important to me. But it was fun while it lasted.

Our home towns are marked with a star. Gösta's town of Lycksele is in the north, and my home village, Dala-Husby, is closer to Stockholm, where we worked and met.

Gösta's Wild Dream

AFTER WE HAD BEEN MARRIED for about five years, Gösta shared a dream he had always had. He said, "Before I met you, I wanted to go to another country. Maybe Brazil or America."

"Gösta? *Nejmen* (but no)!" I couldn't believe that Gösta had such a wild dream.

I asked him, "Where would you go today if you had a chance?"

"I think I would go to America," he said. "Would you like to?"

"Yes, that would be nice. Could we do it?"

"Well, we don't have any children. And we could sell the restaurant and take a trip and see something else while we are young."

Gösta wanted to see the world, and we had nothing holding us back. He knew that one of us could find work, and the immigration quota was never filled for Sweden.

That's all he had to say. My head started to spin, and I couldn't stop thinking about this. Every day I had different feelings. Should we go? Should we sell the cafe, or should we get a manager to run it? We were so full of emotions, but now there was no turning back.

We asked the U.S. Embassy for instructions on how to get our visas, and were told: "You need two good recommendations from honest, important men; you need to show that you have enough money to support yourselves for a length of time; and you need enough money to return to Sweden. If you have all of that, you can get visas."

I came up with a scheme to get the two recommendations. As part of our business in the cafe, we brought coffee to the people at Rådhuset (the courthouse). They would place an order by phone. We would then send over a *brickflicka*. She carried a basket with a pot of coffee, cups and saucers, cream and sugar, sandwiches, sweet rolls, and cigarettes. She had to get there fast so the coffee, in a china pot, didn't get cold.

On a day that I knew one of the high judges would be in, I decided to go there myself and see what I could do. They had the usual order, so I brought the food and cigarettes over and made a big deal of serving them as nicely as possible.

They said, "Oh, there's a new *brickflicka* today. While you're here you might as well take back the dirty dishes. The regular girl says Mrs. Bergström is nagging and nagging her about them."

"Oh, does Gun Britt say that? I understand the owner can be that way. And what about the *kupongs* (coupons)?" It was after the war and there were still shortages, so people needed coupons for meat, coffee, bread, butter, and cigarettes.

"Oh, we never give the regular girl any coupons. She doesn't ask us for them, so we just forget it."

I said, "Well, I can tell you, I am Mrs. Bergström." I thought they would go under the table! "And now I have a way you can pay me back for all those coupons. I need letters of recommendation from two honest people in order to go to America. Can you do that for me?"

"Oh, sure, sure, we can do that. Just bring them in and we'll sign them right away."

After that, it took two months for our papers to be ready, only two months, that was all. So that is how we got our letters.

America—
Here We Come

WE RECEIVED OUR VISAS and sold our cafe on the same day. We made arrangements to let another young couple rent our apartment and use our furniture.

And now we had to say goodbye to our families. We went to Dalarna to my home. And to Lappland to Gösta's parents' home. That was difficult because Gösta's parents didn't want us to leave. "You should go to the doctor and have your head examined!"

They were pious Christians, and Gösta's mother was crying as we prayed and sang a hymn together. She said, "If you ever hear this song in America, think of us." Yes, of course, we would.

On the second Sunday we were in America, we went to a Swedish church in Brooklyn. The first hymn we sang was that one. I could not sing; I was crying all the way through it. "Shall We Gather at the River" was the hymn, and I felt like it was a greeting from her.

The day we were to leave for America was a gray, snowy day, January 31, 1947. When we went to the Central Station to take the train to Göteborg, everyone seemed so somber. We knew why we were sad, but why were all these people sad?

It turned out that this was the day that the body of Crown

The *Gripsholm* sailed between Sweden and America from 1927 to 1954, except for the war years. We thought it was so big and beautiful.

Prince Gustav Adolf (the father of the current king) was due to arrive at the train station. He had been in Holland hunting with his friend, Prince Bernhard, of the Netherlands. On the way home, his plane crashed over Denmark. The prince left a wife and five children. It was so sad.

We boarded the train and were lulled into quietness by the swaying of the train. The clitter-clatter of the wheels became a rhythm to the words of a song in my head, *Mor, lilla mor, vem är väl som du ingen i hela världen* (Mother, dear Mother, there is no one in the whole world like you). Over and over I heard those words. And I missed my sister and brother and father.

My sister cried so hard as we left and later told me she had a sore throat from it all. When would we see them again? Letters take ten days by air mail. Telephone calls cost so much. This is so hard. I wish I could go back and give them all an extra hug.

Soon we were in Göteborg. Our ship was beautiful—so white and big. We were excited now and all we could think about was to get on the boat and see what our room was like. The cabin was small but pleasant, and it had bunk beds, a desk, and a closet. What an adventure!

As the ship was leaving the port, Gösta and I went up on the top deck, hand in hand with tears in our eyes. We watched the *Vinga fyr* (the lighthouse, and the last sight for ships leaving Göteborg) get smaller and smaller, and the seagulls that were following us finally said goodbye. We had each other, and everything would be all right.

I had bought three new dresses, and Gösta had a new tuxedo for the captain's dinner. I also had a new evening gown, but I used it only once because of my seasickness. I had a suit from one of the best French tailors in Stockholm, a red velvet coat, a gray hat, and several skirts.

Since we had sold our business, we had a little extra money. *Ja*, I had some wonderful things. My evening gown was light blue with a layer of white lace ruffles over it. I wore it to the captain's dinner but never used it after that. A few years later it was no longer in style, so I used it as a nightgown and felt very fancy

On the deck of the ship, I am seated at the left of Gösta. We enjoyed being with the other passengers. This photo was taken on our second trip to America.

as I went to bed. Clothes I had, I must say.

When I was in Stockholm with my grandmother, she had taken me to a fortune teller once when I was about seventeen. I remember what he said: "One day you are going to a country far away, over a big water. If the weather is bad when you reach the coast, you may as well go home because nothing is going to go right. But if the sun is shining, then you can be happy, because you will have the key to a good future, and everything will go well for you."

As I sat on the deck chair of the *Gripsholm*, the weather was terrible. I was worried. People from Dalarna are a little bit superstitious. And I thought, now we have really done something!

But when we arrived in New York after ten days at sea, at 11:00 a.m. on February 11, the sun was high in the sky, and I thought, we can feel at home right away. Everything is going to go well for us.

And with a big smile Gösta and I got off the ship.

New York,
New Adventures

COMING OFF THE SHIP with us was a juniper smoked ham, supposedly the best ham in the world, sent with us from friends of friends in Dalarna. We were to bring it to a musician, Erik Olsson, in Brooklyn. Food is important to Swedes! A woman met us at the dock to take the ham to the man. But we didn't have anything to give her because the customs authorities had taken it.

She then asked if we had made a phone call to reserve a room, and of course we hadn't done that. She said, "Okay, you can stay with me. I have a bungalow and you can rent an apartment there for the time being."

Well, now, I remembered that bungalows were what the movie stars lived in. I had read that in *Film Journalen*, a movie magazine. I thought, that's good enough for us. She said we'd better take a taxi because it was quite far out. Her home was on Long Island, actually on Coney Island, by the ocean.

We took our eleven clumpy bags, new suitcases that would be museum pieces today, into the little house. It was nothing like the film stars' bungalows! This one had two small apartments, and they shared a bathroom. When you wanted to use it, you would lock the other renters' door, but you had to remember to unlock it when you were done. Well, we didn't remember to do that on our first day. We went into the city, came home at night, and then found out what we had done.

We had brought some of our precious belongings from Sweden with us. One reason was to have familiar things around, but I also think we thought of them as insurance. We had heard that we could sell things and get good money for them. Sweden is famous for its crystal, and we had five crystal vases. They are valuable antiques now.

We also had three paintings. One of them reminded us of Gösta's father, and we still have it. We were shopping in Gamla Stan (Old Town) in Stockholm one Christmas, and while we were enjoying the *julmarknad* (Christmas market), we saw a painting in the window of Peterssons Konsthandel (art dealer's shop). I said, "Gösta! That looks just like your father when he reads the Bible!"

"*Ja*," he said.

"Would you like it?"

"*Ja*, I would, would you like it?"

This painting that looked exactly like Gösta's father reading the Bible came with us to America. We still love it.

"*Ja*, I would, too."

I went to that store myself one day and bought the painting for Gösta. On Christmas Eve, as we began to open our presents, Gösta said, "Ingrid, I went to get that painting for you, but someone had already bought it, so I bought you tea cups instead."

"Gösta, don't tell me that. It's like you have already opened my presents for me. . . . Did they tell you who bought it?"

"No, they didn't know."

After we finished opening presents, I told Gösta to pick up the red thread that was on the floor. Why? Because you need to follow it. Gösta did as he was told and followed the thread out the door of our apartment. There in the hallway was a big package. And inside was the painting. It really did look just like his father, reading his Bible by candlelight. We have it hanging in our dining room to this day.

Those were some of the things we packed with us and never said goodbye to. Yes, we had taken so much with us, plus the juniper smoked ham.

While we were still in Stockholm, Gösta had studied a map of New York, so he knew the addresses of all the places we wanted to visit. He has always had a good sense of direction, a built-in compass in his head. All I had to do was follow him. We went to department stores, shows, and Radio City. Oh, we will never forget the Rockettes at beautiful Radio City! We had never seen anything like it. It was a memory to last a lifetime.

One day we tried coffee from something new called an automat machine. I thought the coffee was awful. We were used to drinking coffee from china cups.

We had taken a taxi to our new home the first day, but we had no idea how to get there on public transportation. So we went into a mom-and-pop store at closing time and asked for directions. The pop, who was at least eighty-five years old, closed the store and said he would go with us and help us find our place. We had to change buses three times. When we got to our apartment, the man wouldn't take any money. How could we pay him back?

I was impressed by Rockefeller Center when we were getting to know New York City.

Only by helping others in similar situations, and we have tried to do that through the years.

There were so many people in the city, and so many nationalities. We thought everyone was very friendly. I noticed that the women weren't as well-dressed as the women in Stockholm, and the American women wore so much make-up! The newspapers were so big and cost only two cents. We had no problem figuring out the money, but English we had to work on.

Gösta had learned some English in school, and he had listened to American radio programs such as "Lum and Abner." It wasn't easy to buy a radio so soon after the war, but we found one with a crack in it at Macy's, and listening to the radio helped us learn English. We had that radio for fifteen years.

We explored the city every day for a week. Then it was time for us to look for jobs.

Learning American Ways at a
Swedish Restaurant

ONE DAY when we were eating at the Three Crowns Restaurant on East 54th Street in Manhattan, I said to Gösta, "I think I would like to work here."

So I asked if they would have a job for me. "No, we don't have anything open." I continued talking to them, and we had a pleasant conversation. The manager then left for a time, and when he came back he said, "We're going to make a job for you. You come in here tomorrow, and we'll help you."

They had a *smörgåsbord* (buffet table) invention that had been at the 1939-40 New York World's Fair. It had two levels and moved in a big circle. A third of it was behind a wall in the pantry. It would come out full of food, and when it went back in, someone would refill the plates so it always looked good. Well, that was the job they had for me—to see that the *smörgåsbord* always looked perfect.

They also wanted me to put crushed ice on the plates for the oysters, and I got extra tips for that. I worked six days a week and made $50.00 plus, and I could eat the best food you could dream about. That was good pay for 1947.

But I wanted to be one of the waitresses and be with the customers. Famous people would come in, and I couldn't see anything from behind the wall of the *smörgåsbord*.

When I asked if I could be a waitress, they said, "No, you don't speak English well enough." I said, "Then I think I might look for a job at the Stockholm Restaurant." They said, "Well, okay, tomorrow you can try the dining room for lunch, and if you aren't good during lunch, we will send you back to the pantry for dinner time."

I was assigned to help Ture, who worked in the balcony above the *smörgåsbord*. I was to bring the food to him, clean the tables, and learn what it was all about. That day a Norwegian man came in, and he could speak Swedish with me. I told him that the boss said I needed to do a good job or I would be sent back to the kitchen.

The Norwegian man then said, "Here is ten dollars. Don't keep it, give it to the fellow, Ture, and he's going to tell your boss that you are terrific!" That's what happened, so I was able to continue there.

It took maybe two or three weeks, and then I got my own station. My first two customers were Catholic priests. I was feeling sure of myself because the chef had told me that the first thing I

The Three Crowns Restaurant was famous for its revolving *smörgåsbord*, located behind the center rows of tables. I learned a lot working here.

serve should be old-fashioned bean soup. You start with that.

Okay, I can do this.

Well, the priests said, "We will have two Old Fashioneds." I went to the kitchen and got two cups of bean soup. When I served them the soup, they said, "What is this?"

"Old-fashioned bean soup," I said. And they said, "No, that is not what we want." Then another waiter, Sven, came over and said, *"Nu är det kokta fläsket stekt"* (Now the boiled pork is fried, meaning now you're really in trouble). He thought what I had done was terrible. It was cocktails they wanted. In the first place, I didn't think priests would drink, and, second, I had never heard of those drinks. But the rest of the evening went well, and I stayed at the restaurant for a year and enjoyed working there.

Another day I was going to take my first lobster out of the shell for a customer. I didn't know they had cut it loose in the kitchen and that I was just to remove it. I had the lobster in a napkin on one hand and a little fork in the other. I poked the fork in and pulled. I was going to make sure I got the meat out by force. Out it came and flew over the customers and landed in the melted butter dish on the next table. I started to laugh and just couldn't stop. Then everyone around started to laugh, too, but not the owner. That day he came close to letting me go.

I also remember serving actress Greta Garbo. Our maitre d' was a friend of hers, and he always called her *"lilla* Greta," which was a sweet name, but she was not small. One time she ordered brown beans and salt pork, and I thought she could have eaten a little better when she was so famous and rich.

Many Swedish businessmen also came to the restaurant. One of them had the same last name as I had, and he was friendly and always sat in my station. Today, his son and his wife are among our best friends.

I also met a Swedish movie star named Marta Toren, whom Sophia Loren named herself after, the story goes. Marta had signed a seven-year contract with Universal Studios and was on her way to Hollywood. We used to talk about some of the friends we had in common back in Stockholm.

She said, "Why don't we meet when you are off between shifts this afternoon." So we went out and had fun in the dime stores. The prices were right. I was always buying things for my family at home in Sweden, and it helped me to be less lonesome for them. And the music in the stores! I remember one song that was a big hit in 1947, "She's Too Fat for Me."

Another time Marta and I went to the drugstore, and she

bought me a vinyl doll. We christened it with 7UP and named it Peter Gynt after the hunter who roamed the mountains for bears and elks in Henrik Ibsen's tale, "Peer Gynt." Then Marta ordered a banana split for me. I had never had one before, so my eyes got big and round.

She also did something else that was in my favor. *Life Magazine* was publishing an article, "A Day in New York with Marta Toren," and she talked the editors into going to the Three Crowns for lunch. That was appreciated by my boss. Sadly, Marta died

I met Swedish actress Marta Toren at the Three Crowns Restaurant, and we became good friends. She encouraged us to move to California.

of a brain disease at the age of only thirty-one.

After about a year, we were ready to leave New York and move on. We were leaving a place that had taught us so much, and we have never forgotten it.

California Calls

WHILE I WAS WORKING as a waitress, Gösta had been working too. Although he had been an experienced accountant in Stockholm, he couldn't get a job in the United States doing the same work, so he had to take whatever job he could find.

He worked for a time at Spaulding's baseball factory. He would handstitch the leather on the baseballs. It was tedious piecework, and he came home every day with bloody hands. He didn't like this job and was so relieved the day I suggested we take Marta up on her invitation and go to California. Another big adventure!

We left by train, and on our way we passed through Chicago. We stayed only one day, and the weather was bad and everything looked gray. We couldn't see the sun, and we thought this was the last place we'd ever want to live.

After Chicago, the train headed south. The train was interesting. Once I asked Gösta what he thought the difference was in the bathrooms for people of a different color. My curiosity was too much, and I had to go in one. There was no difference, and that made me feel better.

Then we got stuck in a snowstorm. We were on the Kansas prairie on the tracks for twenty-seven hours. That was a big news story. Everything was frozen, and we didn't have any food and

I tried to pose California-style on the beach in Santa Monica! We liked California, but Gösta couldn't find a job there.

couldn't use the bathrooms.

There was an older couple facing us in the same car. They were eating all the time—German bread, sausages, and ham, and nobody else had any food. But I would have died of hunger before I asked them for any. That time we didn't appreciate German food, but today it is one of our favorites.

Our next stop was El Paso, Texas. After gray Chicago, after snow in Kansas, after German ham, it was wonderful to step off the train and smell oranges. We had never seen an orange tree before, and Texas seemed so beautiful.

As Swedes from the north, we get lonesome for the sun and heat. It was warm in Texas, and Gösta said, "Now we should go and buy some nice summer clothes." So he bought a new pair of pants, and I bought some summery things, too. We checked into the Knox Hotel, changed into our new clothes, and went to dinner.

After dinner, when we were ready to leave, Gösta tried to get up from his chair. His new pants were stuck to the underside of the table. I looked under the table and said, *"milda makter"* (holy Moses)! Gösta, you are stuck to a hundred chewing gums. The owner came over and felt so bad. He treated us to the dinner, and he promised to pay for cleaning, but the pants were never nice-looking again.

Our next stop was Phoenix, Arizona. It seemed like a small town at that time, and we liked it so much because most of the houses were white, and it was so sunny and bright.

On to southern California, where I thought I had a job waiting for me. The owner of Bit of Sweden on Sunset Boulevard in Hollywood had come into the Three Crowns in New York one night. He said, "If you ever come to California, you can have a job with us at Bit of Sweden."

Well, I took him seriously, so I went there and, of course, they didn't have any openings. He looked at me and said, "I did say you could have a job?" "Yes, you did," I said. "You come in tomorrow, and we will arrange for you to work." They served *smörgåsbord*-style there, and it was such a big place that they could always use the help.

But Gösta couldn't find a job. The war was over, and the soldiers were first in line for jobs. Once they found out how nice the weather was in California, they wanted to stay. And the film industry was changing back from its wartime function, so it was going to take time for the job market to improve.

But I was working. Being in Hollywood, I would often see famous people. I remember one little man who said, "I like Sweden because lingonberries grow there." And I thought, "Why would you like a country because of some berries?" Every time he came in, he wanted a large spoonful on his plate.

One day he told me, "I have a son and he has a very good voice. He can really sing!" I thought to myself, here we go again.

Because I was young, people would sometimes get the idea that I should meet their son, not knowing that I was married. The man said, "His name is Bing, and my name is Crosby." I thought, well, if he can sing, good for him. Later on I learned who Bing Crosby was, and to this day I think of that little man whenever I hear "White Christmas." The man was right, his son had a good voice.

But Gösta couldn't find a job in California, and when the promoters said, "Go west, young man," where else was there to go? So Gösta said, "I think we have to go to Chicago; I hear they have jobs." And I thought to myself, "Oy, yoi, yoi, that is bad!"

Chicago Interlude

WE RETURNED TO CHICAGO, and Gösta got a job as a bartender at Harding's Restaurant downtown. At that time, I don't think he'd ever tasted a cocktail. He learned to mix drinks, and it didn't take him long to become an expert in making Manhattans and Martinis. He had the recipes above him on a lampshade, and he referred to them when necessary.

I got a job at the Kungsholm Restaurant, and that was both good and bad. This restaurant had the puppet opera, very famous at the time. The line to get in was often long, even with reservations. I was assigned to the third floor, in the opera room.

At first I thought it was the nicest room, until I found out they didn't have a *hiss* (dumbwaiter) to bring the food up from the basement-level kitchen. So it was forty-eight steps down to get the food and forty-eight steps back up with the trays to serve the customers. It was very difficult, but we had nice customers.

One woman working there had come up from Arkansas to earn money because she couldn't earn this kind of money in her home town. Her son had died in the war, and she wanted to order a beautiful headstone for his grave. The restaurant owner thought her story was so touching that one night he mentioned it to a special customer. The man heard the story, took out his checkbook, and wrote a check for the whole amount. The cus-

The puppet opera was a big attraction at the Kungsholm restaurant, where I had to carry the food up and down 48 steps.

tomer was Clark Gable, and we all liked him so much after that.

One day I decided I couldn't take it any longer. Forty-eight steps is a long way, especially when carrying a big tray of food on your shoulder. Before I reached the last few steps, I fainted, with five ducklings on my tray, and that was the end of the opera restaurant for me!

Today, the puppet opera is on display at the Museum of Science and Industry in Chicago. You can press a button and see one of the operas that was once shown at the Kungsholm Restaurant.

One More Time
for Sweden

AFTER TWO-AND-A-HALF YEARS in America, we decided to return to Sweden. Our parents were overjoyed that we were coming home. We took the *Kungsholm* back, and I wasn't seasick this time and enjoyed the trip.

When we arrived in Göteborg, the passengers were greeted by a band and people screaming "Welcome home." It was a fantastic feeling. My mother and father, who had been driven all the way in a friend's taxicab, were waiting on the shore to welcome us, and because of the big day my father had a straw hat on his head. Here we were, back in our home country, and this crowd is welcoming us! The sun was so beautiful.

At that time it was very special to return. Today you can make the trip in seven or eight hours, and you can go so often that you wonder if your relatives and friends get tired of seeing you.

We moved back into our apartment on Agnegatan in Kungsholmen in Stockholm. Next we went to our cafe and tried to buy it back, but the owners didn't want to sell it. Now what should we do?

We had a friend in the real estate business. He said, "I know about a *konditori* that is for sale." A *konditori* was a place that is

fancier than a cafe where they sell coffee and pastries at a count-
er. They were, and still are, very popular in Sweden. We also
noticed an ad for a waitress at this *konditori*. So I said to Gösta, "I
think I'm going to ask for a job there, and I will see right away if
the business is good!"

Gösta isn't as impulsive as I am, and he wants to take more
time to look into things. But I got a job there right away, thinking they wanted to sell. The *konditori* was on Tegelbacken by the
train station. The owner's wife would come in almost every
morning for coffee. She was the opera star, Birgit Nilsson, who
became world famous. She had nothing to do with the business,
but her husband would come in often.

When I found out that the rumors were wrong, that they did-
n't want to sell, I quit. And then we went back to America. Years
later I called Birgit Nilsson when she was in Chicago and told
her the story and invited her to come over for coffee. She didn't
remember me, but it was fun to talk to her.

Even though we tried to buy a business and stay in Sweden,
we realized that we both really wanted to return to America. We
had felt that we needed to try our best to stay, because Gösta's
parents especially wanted us to. Sometimes I think about this.
How could we leave our parents when they were so sad? Today
it is a different story, when travel is so much faster.

Back then, a one-minute telephone call cost a fortune, and
we had to order it ahead of time. If I could have called my mother like I could call my brother and sister in recent years, that
would have been so nice. But in those years, as soon as I heard
my mother's voice, I would spend a few dollars crying for awhile.
Then when I would talk, she would start crying. We didn't get
much talking done, but at least we heard each other's voices.

We were in Sweden for almost a year, but we didn't spend
much time looking for a restaurant to buy. Gösta worked as an
accountant, and I took it easy.

Back in Chicago
for New Adventures

IT WAS 1950, and we were going back to America for the second time. We really liked everything about living in America. But now where do we go, New York? Or Chicago, where we had started to make good friends? We flipped a coin. *Krona eller klave* (heads or tails). Chicago won, and we felt that this was the right place for us.

After arriving on the *Kungsholm* in New York, we bought tickets on a Greyhound bus. A man from Dalarna, Carl Eric Wickman, who lived fairly close to my hometown, had started Greyhound, and it became a large and successful company in the United States. When we got off the bus in Chicago, Gösta was sick. There was a draft where he had been sitting, and his ankle and knee were swollen. He was in bed for a couple of months.

In the meantime, I went to work at Bit of Sweden on Rush Street. This restaurant served both dinners and a *smörgåsbord*, but most people ordered the *smörgåsbord*. We were open from 4:00 to 10:00 p.m. and could be out of there by 11:00 p.m. Those were wonderful hours, since we had most of the day to ourselves. It was a popular place, and I made good money.

One day, one of the women there said, "I don't think you could get a job in an American place, and if you did, I don't think you'd last more than a couple of days." She thought my accent was too strong.

"You don't think I could make it?"

"No. . . and you should have been here during the Depression. . . ." This was a story I heard all the time, that I was so lucky to be there at that time.

I had the next Monday off, and I went downtown to the Hilton Hotel. It was called the Stevens then. I thought that would be the most beautiful place I could work, and I would show them! I also knew I wouldn't get very far if I went to the employment office. They would have me sit down and fill out an application, and that would not do much good. So I went in and asked for the head hostess.

After talking to her, she said, "Oh, yes, you can start a week from today."

Now I had a job, and when I went back and told the others, they said, "Well, now, you won't last."

But I stayed with that job, even though I hated it that first week. Everything seemed so difficult. When people from the

The Conrad Hilton was called the Stevens Hotel when I first went to work there. It was a glamorous place, where I met and waited on many famous people.

south would order, I had no idea what they wanted. If they said they wanted "foamed" eggs, it meant they wanted a four-minute egg, "formed." And they'd ask for "grits." Couldn't they say "*gröt*"? And sometimes the room-service waiters would take my toast and they'd take the eggs I was supposed to serve.

There was no end to how difficult it was. I would cry when I got home. But I would not give up. I had to be dressed and ready for work at 7:00 a.m., a time that I would usually be sleeping, and then go all the way downtown from the North Side.

The Hilton Hotel dining room was a glamorous place. There were marble statues of famous people around the edge of the room, sort of Italian in design, and white tablecloths. The waitresses wore deep purple uniforms and white aprons.

I waited on Conrad Hilton himself once. He had soup and told me it was delicious but it could have been warmer. I said I could go and get some more, but he said, no, just tell the chef that it was good but it wasn't hot enough. "I'm glad it was me," he said, "and not a paying guest." He was like that, a very nice person.

I also saw Elizabeth Taylor when she came in with Conrad Hilton's son. We exclaimed over her beautiful violet eyes. Today I guess anyone can have eyes that color, with contact lenses, but at that time no one had seen eyes like hers. People said when she divorced Hilton, she got so many stocks that you could lay them out next to each other and they would go around the block. If that's true, I don't know.

I was working a lot and making good money, and Gösta told me a funny thing to say. He said, "if anyone asks you what you are going to do with all your money, just tell them you're going to give it to the poor; would you like to put your name on the list?"

Well, one day after working the breakfast and lunch shifts, I came back that night to work a party. The bartender must have thought I was working too much, so he said, "What are you going to do with all your money?" I decided that now I would be

funny. I said, "I'm going to give it to the poor, would you. . . ."
He got so mad that he threw a big drink with ice cubes in my
face. The ice got in my eyes. He was then told not to be mean to
me, and he left me alone. It isn't easy to catch on to what is funny
and what isn't in a new country.

My boss, Miss Robinson, would sometimes greet me by asking, "How are you?" I would tell her if I had a headache or was
tired or how I actually felt. She told me not to say all that because
in America "How are you?" means the same as "Hello." I was
learning a lot about American ways.

One day a distinguished couple came into the restaurant, and
they were assigned to my station. Miss Robinson saw this and got
excited and said, "Oh, Ingrid, do you know how to be polite in
English?"

What I thought to myself I won't say!

"Oh, yes, I will be very quiet. I'll just smile."

"Good, good, that man is such a big shot."

So when I went over to the table where Mr. and Mrs.
Richard Nixon were sitting, he said, "What did she tell you? That
must have been very important."

"She told me you are a big shot."

"So, is that what she said!"

Then he started to talk to me and said I reminded him of the
Swedish girl who acted in the movie, *I Remember Mama*.

The next day, my boss was watching to make sure they didn't
put anyone in my station who shouldn't be there. And here
comes Richard Nixon and his wife. He asked to be put in the
Swedish girl's area. I was very proud, I was. After that my boss
would seat anyone in my area.

Famous people came through Chicago and into the Hilton
Hotel all the time. John Wayne (I say Yon Vain if I'm not careful)
was in town once for something political. He enjoyed talking to
me and teasing, and I was a little bolder with him because he
seemed to like that. The others would tell me to watch out, I
could become Mrs. John Wayne, the fourth, but it wasn't any-

thing like that. He was just lots of fun.

When Doris Day came to the hotel, I had the chance to wait on her. She ordered ice cream. Since that's all she said, I brought her vanilla. Well, she wanted chocolate, and she asked so nicely. So when I brought her the chocolate in a silver dish, I guess it hadn't been rinsed thoroughly and smelled like bleach. I felt badly for her, but she was as nice in person as in her movies.

One day one of the waitresses said, "There are some Swedish people who heard we have a Swedish waitress, and they want to see you."

I went over to greet them. I had thought the man was an old shoemaker when I had seen him come down the stairway that morning. I was sure he was there for Shoemakers' Week at the Hilton. The woman with him said, "I'm sure you know who this gentleman is?"

"Well," I said, "I am 99 percent sure, but why don't you tell me?"

"This is Carl Milles." Of course, one of Sweden's most beloved sculptors!

When my shift was over, I stayed awhile and talked to him. He was sitting off to one side, writing a letter to his wife with green ink. As we talked, he said, "When you come to Sweden some day, I will invite you over, and I will invite the king, too, and we can all have coffee together." A nice thought, I felt. Then he said, "I'm going to give you $10.00; go buy something from me. I remember what it was like to do this job. I was a waiter in Paris when I studied there."

He also said, "I would like to treat you and your husband for dinner tomorrow. When I come down for breakfast in the morning, we can decide where to go. It would be nice to meet with you both in private." I went home and called my friends and said, "We are going out for dinner with Carl Milles!"

Morning came, and no Carl Milles. Lunch, and no Carl Milles. I still believed what he had said, even though he never showed up. Six months later I received a letter from Italy, seven pages long in green ink. He was laid up after falling off a stepladder, and he had his legs "up in the air." Then he explained that the day he was going to meet us, they came for him at 5:00 a.m. and took him to the airport by police escort so he could get to the United Nations in New York, where some of his sculptures were going to be installed.

Two years later, we visited Stockholm, and I said to Gösta, "How about if we call up Carl Milles and see if he remembers me? Maybe he doesn't, but I wanted to find out if he meant what he had said." So I called, and the woman who had been with him in America answered. "Oh, he would like to see you, but he's in Växjö for a meeting. But he'll be back. Why don't you come here on Friday, around 4:00 p.m., and bring your husband."

Yes, we would be there. His home and the sculpture park are just outside Stockholm in Lidingö, a famous place he has. He welcomed us with open arms, and called me "little Ingrid." He said, "Why didn't you give us your phone number when you called so we could reach you? The king was here yesterday for coffee!" Carl Milles had celebrated his eightieth birthday, and the king wanted to help him celebrate. That was the grandfather of the current king.

And Carl Milles said, "You will eat from the same cake; he didn't eat the whole thing." A lady from Old Town had baked sweet rolls and a big beautiful cake that said, "Carl 80 years old." And he said to Gösta, "Take another roll; the king had two." "Oh, he had?" Gösta said. "Then I'll take two, also." We had so much fun with this. He told us we should call him Uncle Carl or *Farbror* (father's brother) and his wife, Aunt Olga. A visitor came while we were there, and Carl told us, "He lives in Stockholm; he can wait or he can come back another day."

Later on, after Carl's death, I was invited to join his wife for tea. Her health wasn't good, so I only had a few minutes with her. She told me that *Farbror* Carl liked me so much, and then she took my hand so sweetly. She died the next day. But we were so pleased that Carl Milles had kept his word.

Back to the Hilton in Chicago. "Lunch at the Hilton" was a live radio interview show, starring Tony Weitzel, a *Chicago Daily News* gossip columnist. I served the tables for that show for a year-and-a-half. This show brought extra publicity for movie stars when they were opening a movie in Chicago. They were invited to perform on stage at the movie opening, and they would go to the Hilton and be interviewed during the lunch hour. Most of them stayed at the Hilton, too.

The first one who came in was Barbara Hutton. And then Eddie Fisher, and, of course, Anita Ekberg. She was so beautiful that the men forgot what they were doing and just looked at her. She looked stunning in a pleated gray skirt and a gray sweater. She showed me a card inviting her to Eisenhower's inauguration, and she was proud of that.

This period of time was wonderful. First we served our regular breakfast station. Then we set up our station for lunch, another girl and I, and waited on the stars. I think the first few weeks I wrote a letter to my sister every day. I told her I didn't think Frank Sinatra was so good-looking, that he bit his nails, that his red flannel shirt was wrinkled. Joan Blondell came down with rollers in her hair and was sent back to her room. When she came down the next time, she really looked like a movie star.

I remember that when Olympic figure skater Sonja Henie came in, she seemed sad about something. Her manager must have said something to her because she seemed sad all the time. She was very beautiful, though.

I made many good friends at that time. One Swede who worked at the Hilton was Lars Felke, who was learning the hotel business under sponsorship of the Scandinavian Foundation. Lars later became the first manager of the Birger Jarl Hotel in Stockholm. Another Swede, Rolf Von Otter, a relative of the famous opera singer, Sofie Von Otter, was working at the nearby Palmer House. We have been good friends with them and their wives through the years.

And, now, of course, my favorite story! There was a famous

chimpanzee at that time who was a star in the Tarzan movies. His name was Cheeta. He recently turned seventy-one and is being cared for in Palm Springs, California.

He was in town for a movie opening, just like a movie star. And he was going to have lunch at the table with others in the Hilton dining room! He got two bananas for his meal and waited to start eating them until everyone got their food. And then he ate really nicely, acting like he was the star at the table. I could hardly believe it.

At the end of the meal, we'd give our guests a finger bowl on a silver platter, with warm water and a lemon slice. I gave a finger bowl to everyone at the table except Cheeta. Do you know what he did? He pinched me on the hip, and looked so mad. Then he put his fingers into a water glass and flicked water at me. Next he picked up his napkin and dried his hands very carefully.

Well, that was one of the most exciting times of my life, to see a chimpanzee do that. It was like he was saying to me, "Why can't I have a finger bowl? Don't you think I know how to use it?"

When Cheeta came in, Miss Robinson wondered, "What kind of monkey business is this?" But his handlers insisted he sit with them at their table. *Ja,* I never forgot him!

There were hundreds of movie stars that I met from that time, and one chimpanzee.

Courtesy of the C.H.E.E.T.A. Primate Foundation.

Waiting on Cheeta at the Hilton Hotel was a special memory for me. Today he is the world's oldest living primate. He is being cared for by a primate foundation, and his "ape-stract" paintings help pay for his care.

Settling Down in Our Own Apartment

WHEN WE RETURNED to the States the second time in 1950, it was common to live in a boarding house. It had furnished apartments that were rented on a temporary basis.

We lived in one for a year until we got our first two-bedroom apartment, which was located on North Ridge Avenue. It was unfurnished, and Gösta thought it was too big. He still wasn't sure we were staying in America, and it made him nervous to think we'd have to buy furniture for a living room, kitchen, dining room, and two bedrooms. But I said I could do it.

"How much can I spend?"

"Well, I don't know. We have to be careful."

"Just give me a number, and I will do it for that."

"How about $500.00?"

I thought I could do it for that. So I looked in the newspaper for used furniture and saw an ad from a doctor who was moving to Africa. A friend and I went to his place, and the first thing I saw I fell in love with. It was a glass table with a brass pedestal. It was $225.00 without chairs. I couldn't resist it. So now we had a table, but I had spent almost half of my budget.

Next I went to Sears and bought six chairs for $13.00 each. We found an ad for a Wilton rug for $25.00. I thought it was a real Wilton but found out later it wasn't. And at that lady's house I also bought a signed Italian statue, which is in my front entry today, for $15.00. I bought a bed, a mirror, and a few other things. Then the Hilton had one of their sales, something they did for their employees, and I finished furnishing the apartment. I did it for $500.00, and not a penny more. It looked very nice, and we lived there for nearly ten years.

Gösta and I in Chicago at the time of our tenth wedding anniversary.

In the mid '50s, I found out that I had thyroid disease and needed a goiter operation. Gösta had started a new job as manager of the Swedish Engineers' Club, so I could take time off from my job and spend the summer recovering.

There was a man from Sweden staying in our apartment building. Egon Kjerrman was in town with an orchestra for a year, and he had nothing to do during the day since he worked at night. We would do crossword puzzles during the day in Swedish. That man became a popular musician in Sweden and also had charge of music in the military. He would follow the king and queen to other countries and organize music for them.

When I went back to work at the hotel, things seemed very different. I don't know if the operation affected me, but I couldn't carry things like I did before and I was feeling very sensitive. But also some of the excitement was gone because the lunchtime radio station with the movie stars was no longer going on. I only stayed for a couple of months after that.

It did me good to take it easy for awhile, and then I began working at the Svithiod Singing Club on Wrightwood Avenue. The Svithiod Singing Club wasn't fancy like the Hilton, but we enjoyed the friendship of many Swedish Americans who were active there, and I worked there for several years.

Friendships in
Swedish-American Organizations

WE REALLY LIKED CHICAGO now, and this was an exciting time for us. The city wasn't as beautiful as it is today. Mayor Richard M. Daley has made it so beautiful with trees and flowers and ornamental fences.

Chicago was a town where a Swede could really feel at home, because there were so many Swedish organizations, churches with Swedish backgrounds, and cultural activities. I can only mention those we have been involved in.

When we were new in town, there was a group of us who decided we should start our own club. Svenska Gillet (The Swedish Friendship Society) grew from nineteen people at first to hundreds. There was a need for these clubs because the newcomers needed jobs and apartments.

We would help each other in different ways. If someone needed blood, we'd donate blood, or we'd visit someone who might be ill in the hospital, or bring food to a sick person at home. Sometimes Swedes who wanted to emigrate to America needed sponsors, and so some of us would take on that responsibility.

Today, when Swedes come over, they usually have a job before they come or they're married to someone who has a job. Gösta and I were among the first, along with Stina Larson and Britta Seaberg, who were active in Svenska Gillet from its begin-

My sister Signe (left) was visiting us at the time of the thirtieth anniversary of Svenska Gillet.

ning in 1951.

The Swedes who came after us usually had more education and could get better jobs than those who came earlier, and they knew English because Sweden had decided to require it in the schools.

Some of the Swedes who had been here awhile and become successful and well-off could be a little snobbish. I worked in the restaurant business, so that put me in a different class. But I thought it was just a matter of time when we would be on the other side ourselves!

We also supported the local Vasa Lodge and the Independent Order of Svithiod, which has many local chapters. Gösta is still a member of the Verdandi Lodge #3, and I am a member of the Astrid Lodge #65. We've been members since the '50s, and one of the great things about them is that their membership is actually on the rise.

I also became involved with SWEA, Inc., a global network of Swedish women. The letters stand for Swedish Women's Educational Association. This organization has been especially helpful for the younger generation of Swedish-speaking women, and they give stipends for graduate students who study Swedish language and literature. A newcomer from Sweden can call on SWEA to help her feel at home in a new environment. I've been a member for more than twenty years, and it is a great way to stay

The children's museum at the Swedish American Museum Center gives children the chance to pretend they're Swedish pioneers. This child is Stella Magnuson of Seattle, Washington. I'm proud of this museum and all of the staff and volunteers.

in touch with other women who speak Swedish.

Another group I've been involved with is the American Daughters of Sweden. Its focus is to award scholarships at several colleges to young people who want to study Swedish. I've been a member off and on since the 1950s. This group is known for its cookbook, *Swedish Recipes Old and New*, first printed in 1955 but reprinted many times since. The recipes are very accurate. I've never heard a complaint, and I know that the cookbook has sold more than 100,000 copies.

One organization that has been very important to me is the Swedish American Museum Center at 5211 N. Clark Street in Andersonville. It was founded in 1976 by Kurt Mathiasson. The first president was Sven Flodstrom, a contractor, who gave all of his free time for twelve years. Selma Jacobson also helped them continually. She was a Chicago schoolteacher who was a strong and tireless leader in preserving the Swedish heritage in Chicago.

The King of Sweden, Carl XVI Gustav, presided over the official opening of the first museum in a small rented storefront on Clark Street. In 1986 the Board of Directors voted to acquire the old Lind Hardware, a large building where the museum is now located, and in 1988 the Swedish king and queen opened the new museum.

The museum has a gallery for temporary exhibits and a gift shop on the first floor. On the second floor there are offices and exhibits with wonderful artifacts given to the museum to show what life was like for the immigrants in their early years in Chicago. The third floor has a library and classrooms, and a children's museum that shows what life was like in the Old Country. There's a cabin with built-in beds, a farmyard where children can milk a cow and make butter, and a kitchen where they can pretend they're eating fish and potatoes, and much more.

Kerstin Lane, the executive director since 1986, has done a wonderful job of developing the museum center and its many programs and events. Kerstin and her dedicated staff and volunteers have worked very hard, and the museum has become a vital center for Swedish activities in the Chicago area.

I have been a member of the board for a number of years. To me, the museum is a wonderful legacy to give to the Swedish-American community. When many Swedish clubs have closed, it's nice to have a place that will continue to keep our culture and heritage alive to anyone who walks in the door. I wish I could show all of America this museum.

Over the years, we've also supported the Swedish-American Historical Society, which carries on our heritage by publishing a quarterly journal and books on Swedish-American history. The president, Philip Anderson, gives excellent leadership to this scholarly organization. It is so important to preserve written words, too.

The Swedish Central Committee, an umbrella organization that coordinates the activities of more than sixty Swedish-American societies, has for many years sponsored a noontime Lucia program at the City Hall downtown. Many of the Swedish organizations select a young girl to represent them at their Lucia. In order to not have to choose among them, the mayor's representative draws a name, and that girl becomes the official Chicago Lucia.

Swedish-American singing clubs were in their heyday in the '40s and '50s, and there were many male choruses. There were string bands that played in the churches. And musicians from Sweden would come on concert tours. Some presented secular music, and some were singing evangelists. Every time we heard about a concert, we'd try to attend.

We always had a pile of Swedish newspapers and magazines in our home, so we could be informed about Sweden and Swedish-American activities.

There are quite a few churches that continue to celebrate Swedish traditions. We originally attended the Immanuel Lutheran Church in Edgewater, the oldest Swedish-American church in Chicago. Ebenezer Lutheran on Foster Avenue in Andersonville has an annual Lucia program, along with the Swedish American Museum, on December 13. It is so beautiful.

North Park Covenant Church in the North Park neighborhood is the church Gösta and I now belong to. On Christmas morning, at 6:30 a.m. we have a *Julotta* service, and I am often asked to read the Christmas story from the Bible in Swedish. After that, there is a breakfast, all candlelight with beautiful Swedish decorations.

We like the church so much, and the music and singing are fantastic. You cannot find any better musicians than Sharon Peterson at the organ and Charles Olson as choir director. I sometimes think, "Why aren't they all at the opera? The singers are so good."

We used to wonder why members of some of the Swedish-background churches didn't belong to the lodges. We found out that it was because the lodges had dancing and drinking, and many of the church people weren't comfortable there. So they had their social life in their church activities. There is also a temperance society, the Good Templars, who have a park in Geneva, Illinois, where they have Swedish celebrations in the summertime.

But church Swedes and lodge Swedes could all enjoy the many Swedish restaurants in the city of Chicago. I can think of so many that are no longer in business—Villa Sweden, Larson's Restaurant, Idrotts, Sweden House, and the Verdandi that we operated. And we enjoyed many banquets at the elegant Swedish Club on North LaSalle. We were sorry to see it close in 1984.

Belmont Avenue used to have quite a few Swedish stores and

The Tre Kronor Restaurant, on the corner of Foster and Spaulding avenues, is a special place for us, and we eat there often.

On Christmas morning, "God Jul" welcomes us to a beautiful candlelit breakfast after a festive *Julotta* service at North Park Covenant Church.

restaurants, including the original Ann Sather. And Clark Street had Swedish shoe stores, jewelry stores, and travel agencies. We patronized all of them.

Today we still have wonderful stores like Wikstrom's and Erickson's delicatessens in the Andersonville neighborhood. And restaurants like Svea and Ann Sather. Of course we have the Swedish Bakery, too, where we can get *lussekatter* made with saffron, and during Lent we can buy *semlor*, the rolls with almond paste inside and whipped cream on top. We like to eat *semlor* with cinnamon and hot milk, but many Swedes prefer coffee—the stronger the better.

Across Foster Avenue from North Park University is the Tre Kronor restaurant. It has been exciting to follow the young couple who opened it eleven years ago. They bought the restaurant from Kurt Mathiasson, but we owned the building at the time they started.

From the first week, we could see that Patty and Larry Anderson had something special to offer in their restaurant.

Today there is a line waiting to eat every weekend and on a lot of weekdays, too, and they even have to turn people away for their popular Christmas *julbord*. We love going there, and we always run into friends.

That has been our experience in these Swedish-American organizations and activities through the years. Friends and more friends!

Recovering from Cancer and Getting Active Again

ONE DAY DURING THE SPRING of 1960, I went to my doctor, and he told me I had cancer. About that same time, people were talking about Arthur Godfrey, the radio and TV host who had just been diagnosed with cancer, and Secretary of State John Foster Dulles, who had recently died of cancer. People were talking about how terrible it was and how badly they felt for them and their families.

And all the time I had my secret. I had it, too. You just didn't talk about it in those days, and the outlook wasn't nearly as hopeful as it is now. If people heard it, they talked behind me and wouldn't say anything to my face.

But when I went to the hospital for my operation, of course they found out. One woman said, "Oh, Ingrid, Solveig and I have cried all night, we feel so sorry for you! But I tell you, I had a friend, and she lived two years after the operation! So don't you feel bad about it."

Well, she meant well, but it didn't sound good. I remember when they put me to sleep, I kept hearing in my head, two years, two years. I had my surgery on May 13.

In July we drove to Mexico with some friends for a vacation. We had decided we wouldn't talk about my cancer, and I don't think I've ever laughed more in my life. Every day I would go swimming in the ocean, and I got suntanned, and my stomach muscles got strong. When we came home, no one could believe I had been sick because I looked so healthy. That was a good trip.

I recovered from my cancer, but in some ways it changed me forever. As I sat in our apartment, I had thoughts of getting sick again or of dying. My doctor told me I needed to get out and do something.

Gösta was working long hours, both during the day and the evening, as the manager of the elegant and exclusive Swedish Engineers' Club on the near North Side. So to get me out of the apartment, Gösta had me come down and work in the cloak room.

The club was in an old mansion built by a German brewer who hadn't worried about saving money. Lots of mahogany and floor-to-ceiling mirrors with ornate gold frames. The wallpaper, if I can call it that, was made of fabric. One room had big red roses, and another room was decorated in solid silk.

In the 1920s, a group of Swedish engineers bought the house for a private club. There were hundreds of them living and working in Chicago at that time, architects, builders, and engineers. The building had three floors, and they would have their lovely dinners on the third floor where there was a ballroom. They didn't have an elevator, so all of the food and tableware had to be carried up and down again for these parties. It was beautiful but not practical.

The second floor had four rooms, including a library and a parlor. The stairway was the best part of the mansion. It was wide and grand. As you walked up the stairs you were overwhelmed by the magnificently painted glass window on the wall by the stairs. It was quite something.

One day a man was talking to me in the cloakroom. His group was ready to go upstairs for the entertainment, but he didn't join them. I don't know why, but we started talking about books. I asked him if he had ever read *April Snow.*

"And why that book?" he asked.

"Well, because I liked it so much." I told him how happy I was when I found the second book by that author. I kept chatting about it and said, "Oh, you must be tired of hearing me talk about this book."

"Oh, not at all," he said. "Lillian Budd is going to be very happy to hear this!"

I said, "But she will never hear it."

Then he said, "Yes, she will, because I am her secretary."

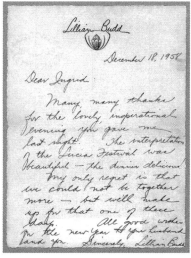

She later wrote to me and said she was happy that I liked her books so much. Gösta then suggested that we invite her to the Engineers' Club for our Lucia evening and *julbord* (Christmas dinner). So we did, and we also met her a couple of times after that.

She had written three books in a series—*April Snow,*

Lillian Budd, one of my favorite authors, sent me this nice thank-you note after attending our Lucia program.

Land of Strangers, and *April Harvest.* Ingrid Bergman wanted to make a movie out of them, but no one would listen to her. Lillian Budd had given her all three books. The first one was signed to Ingrid Lindstrom, the second to Ingrid Rossellini, and the third to Ingrid Schmidt, the names of her husbands.

Nobody could be happier than I when I found the second book. I had wondered for years how one of the main characters, Carl, was doing in Chicago. He had left Sweden for Chicago in the first book, and it is his life in Chicago that the second book is about.

The third book was written after I met Lillian Budd. In a way, she wrote about me in that story. She had a scene about a Lucia party, and it was exactly what she had experienced with us at the

Engineers' Club. Lillian Budd had never been to Sweden, and I couldn't understand how she could write so well about it.

The books were very popular at that time, especially the first one. Lillian Budd received an award from President Eisenhower. Mrs. Eisenhower's grandfather came from Bohuslän, where the story was set, and Lillian Budd would mention that in her speaking engagements.

After working at the Engineers' Club and getting my energy back, I went to work at a steak house on South Wabash Avenue. This was a popular place because the food and the way it was served were unusual.

We were so busy that customers often had to wait an hour for a table. They would wait at the big bar until their name was called. The kitchen was part of the dining room, where the steaks were charcoal-broiled. The dinner consisted of a big lettuce wedge, a baked potato with butter and sour cream, and a tender steak, all for a good price. In the 1950s and '60s, this was something special.

We had to lift the grill off of the charcoal, put the potatoes on it with the steaks, and wheel the cart over to the customers. We knew from the ticket if they had ordered medium or rare. My back was so sore the first week because my muscles weren't used to the lifting.

Sometimes I was a hostess and sometimes a waitress. I noticed that when black people came in the hostesses would print their names so they could seat them away from the front. When white people came they would write their names in script.

That was another one of those things that didn't make any sense to me. I remember wondering what the kitchen chefs, who were mostly black, were thinking. I suppose they didn't say anything because they wanted to keep their jobs. It's hard to believe that this kind of thing was going on in Chicago during those years.

I stayed there until we had the opportunity to buy our own restaurant.

Working Together
in Our Verdandi Restaurant

IN AUGUST OF 1962 we bought the Verdandi Club restaurant at 5015 North Clark Street. The city had just banned *banditer* (slot machines) from restaurants. Slot machines always brought in a lot of money, and when the law was changed to ban them, many clubs and restaurants couldn't make a profit any more.

One of the clubs that couldn't continue was the Verdandi Club, and Gösta and his best friend, Holger Larson, were asked to take it over. So Gösta quit his job as manager of the Engineers' Club.

The restaurant was located in the building owned by the Verdandi #3 of the Svithiod organization. Svithiod had, and still has, many lodges around the country. It was a beautiful building with three floors. Our restaurant was a few steps down, then there was a banquet floor, and the third floor was the hall for the lodge and for renting out.

We worked very hard to make it a good restaurant and hired gourmet chefs and served gourmet food. The first few months were difficult because people didn't know we were there. Our entrance was on the side, so it wasn't seen right away. But as the word spread about our good food, more and more people came, and we got very busy. We had wedding receptions almost every Saturday. We also had a library where we could serve customers

Our Verdandi Restaurant at 5015 North Clark Street had a cozy atmosphere and was decorated in Swedish style.

in a quieter, more private setting.

Our major customer at first was the Wilding Movie Studio. Many of the employees came for lunch, dinner, and cocktails. It was always exciting for us because we never knew what famous people they were going to bring in.

I remember one time when Dana Andrews, a leading man in many American movies, came in and said he wanted *lutfisk*. Well, I knew that unless you grow up eating *lutfisk*, you probably won't like it. I warned him, "You try a little, and if you like it I'll order you a dinner." I gave him a small portion and showed him how to add a little sauce and crushed allspice. And, do you know, he liked it and ordered a full dinner. That was unusual.

Verdandi was a place that reminded people of Sweden. We had a huge painting of Stockholm behind the bar, and we'd play Swedish songs, such as "Hälsa dem där hemma," on our jukebox. Swedes would sit there and think about Sweden and miss it so much. You know, the grass is always greener on the other side.

Word got around to Swedes coming to Chicago that they should come to our restaurant. Sometimes we'd get a call from O'Hare Airport. "We've just landed, and someone told us to come straight to your restaurant." We'd give them our address, and they'd get a cab and come right over.

Every third Friday we'd have a Scandinavian dance. The Swedes, Norwegians, and Danes all came, and the girls could feel comfortable coming by themselves. I can't even guess at the number of couples who are married today who met during those years. Various bands came and played. If they played "I Left My Heart in San Francisco," the whole floor would be full of people dancing. They danced the hambo, schottische, waltzes, and the boogie woogie. Then at about 11:30 p.m. we would treat everyone to coffee and cake.

We were open from 11:00 a.m. until 1:00 a.m. and on Saturdays until 2:00 a.m. We were closed Mondays. If we happened to go in on that day, we'd get stuck doing some kind of

Actor Dana Andrews signed this menu for us after trying his first *lutfisk*. He said he liked it!

work, so it was best to stay away on Mondays.

Gösta managed the place and did the bookkeeping. He kept track of the ordering for the bar and hired bartenders. I might be the "hostess with the mostess" on one day, a waitress another day, and the next day I might be scrubbing toilets. If an employee called to say he or she couldn't come in, I would do that person's job. Being in this kind of business meant doing a little of everything.

We each had our own jobs, but it was nice to be working together at the same place at the same time.

Meeting and Serving
Interesting People

ONE DAY we heard that a famous entertainment group from Swedish TV was in Chicago. I wanted them to come to our restaurant, but I needed to figure out how to get them to come.

I went to the Svithiod Singing Club on Wrightwood Avenue where they were having a reception. I was lucky. I ran right into the arms of singer Rolf Björling, whom I knew well since he was living in Chicago. He was the son of Swedish opera singer Jussi Björling. He took me to where the other musicians were playing, and I said, "You know, I really like your music, but I'm almost tired of it."

"Tired of it? Why?"

"*Ja,* I'm tired of 'Gamla Nordsjön,' of 'Gnesta-Kalle', and Harry Brandelius (a Swedish singer)."

"How can you say you are tired of our music?"

"Well, we have a jukebox with your records at our restaurant, and the customers play them all the time. That is why I'm almost tired of it."

"Where is that restaurant? We should go there."

"Well, if you promise to leave your instruments behind, I will bring a band in for you, and we'll treat you to dinner and a dance."

One man from the group said, "Oh, that is so unusual. They

always say to me, 'My friend is going to have a birthday, so don't forget your violin.'"

I invited them to come when the cocktail party that the Swedish Consul General was giving for them was over. They were there by 8:00 p.m., every one of them. And they had such a wonderful evening.

We were usually closed on Mondays, but on one particular Monday we had a party for sixty people. We were working long and hard to take care of the party, since we were going to a dinner for Prince Bertil of Sweden at the South Side Swedish Club.

Before we could get out the door, a man came in and said, "I have greetings from Sweden." That was nice, but we were in such a hurry. He greeted us from Gärda Edin, a friend of ours. Then he asked where we were going that evening. I told him we were going to a dinner in Prince Bertil's honor.

He said, "Will you tell him hello from me."

"I can't do that."

"You just say, 'Hovmarskalk Johansson says hello,' in Swedish." *Hovmarskalk* is a marshall of the court for the royal family.

I said, "We can't do that because we stand in a line, they say our name, and we just pass by, maybe shake hands."

He said, "We used to make dinners together quite often, the prince and I. He likes food, and he likes to be in the kitchen. Please, I want him to know I'm here."

I promised I would try. I was nervous and didn't know if it was the right thing to do. When it was our turn, I kind of whispered, "Hovmarskalk Johansson hälsade."

"Oh, *tusan* . . . . Is he in town?" He said this really loud. And then turned around and saw that everyone had heard him. We had a good seat for the dinner, with only one table between us. I noticed he looked over at us a few times, probably wondering how we knew this Johansson.

At our restaurant, W. Clement Stone of Combined Insurance Company was one of our favorite customers. He was a businessman who started from nothing and believed in the power of a positive mental attitude. He became a great success and was a generous philanthropist who died a few years ago at the age of 100 years.

Each Friday we'd have forty people from Combined Insurance. There would be a pep talk for the salesmen, sometimes from Mr. Stone himself. I learned a lot when I listened in. Once I heard him say that if you have a problem, don't ask your friend or the person you work with, but go to the top.

Each year they would bring about 150 people to our Christmas *smörgåsbord*. We served a wonderful *julbord*. The food tables would take up a whole room. We had one evening for the Verdandi Club members and other evenings for various organizations that made reservations.

We would drape the tables with white and royal blue cloths and place candles and beautiful Swedish Christmas decorations in the middle. Then we would arrange our many different food specialties. I would wear my national costume and have my picture taken by the table.

One year we didn't get a reservation from Clement Stone, and I wondered why. Then I remembered what he had said. I decided I'm going to call him and see if he practices what he preaches.

It was very difficult to get a hold of him, but finally he was on the phone. I told him I wanted to know the reason I didn't get his business this year. He was very nice and said, "I don't know anything about this, but I'm going to find out!" Someone from the company called back that afternoon and made a reservation.

We also had some exposure to politicians during those years. When they want votes, they go to different restaurants and clubs. If they went to a herring breakfast with Swedes, they might pick up some votes.

One time Richard J. Daley, the first Mayor Daley, came to the lodge above our restaurant for a herring breakfast. I was asked to serve him the spirits, aquavit. So he called me "the girl with the spirit."

I wanted him to come to our restaurant, and he said, "Someday I'll be back here for lunch." I saw him in public settings a few times, and he'd say, "I'll be over to eat in your restaurant."

I got tired of him saying that, so I told him, "Don't tell me that Mayor Daley is coming, because you don't mean it." He crossed himself and said he would come. Sidney Olson, the Cook County recorder of deeds, commented, "Now he will come, he crossed himself, he has to." And he did, and signed a menu for us acknowledging his visit.

I even had a chance to bring some *glögg* to his house on the South Side. Gösta had a special recipe that everyone loved. A friend of the mayor, Colonel Jack Reilly, the city's director of special events, would come in with his wife on Fridays for our white fish, so he asked us to bring some of Gösta's special *glögg* to his friend, the mayor, on Christmas Eve. I think I frowned at first, knowing that this was our only day off. But Colonel Reilly was a good customer, and I could never say no to a good customer. He said, "Do that. Bring some to him, a couple of bottles at least."

So we went down to South Lowe. It was snowing, and we went around noon, Gösta and I. "I'll go in, Gösta, I want to see him." I picked up the box and opened the car door. All of a sudden I was surrounded by security guards. They had come out of the bushes and from the sides of the house, holding things that looked like baseball bats.

They said, "What do you have in there?"

I said, "I have Sveeedish *glögg*." I pronounced it funny. "What are you going to do with that?" I told them the story. They asked me who sent it, and I told them Colonel Reilly did. "Well, why didn't he bring it himself?"

"Well, he is not here. He and his wife, Herta, are in Arizona." I made sure to mention his wife's name.

"Give it to me then," one of them said.

"Well, I would like to give it myself."

"No, we'll give it to him."

"Make sure he gets it today. It's Christmas Eve, so he needs it today." They did give it to him that day, I found out later.

Colonel Reilly was a Democrat, and we had a lot of Republicans come into our restaurant. I tell you, I couldn't tell the difference. One time he said, "You know when you introduce your friends to me, you should make sure they are Democrats." I guess that day I had introduced him to a Republican. But I think he was kidding, more or less.

One of the groups that met regularly at Verdandi was the Chicago Swedish Male Chorus. Every Tuesday night they rehearsed in our banquet hall. They had good soloists like Karl-Erik Olsson, Hans Bolling, and Richard Young. I liked to stand by the closed door and listen to their beautiful voices. They often gave concerts and sang at big events.

Our friend, Gunnar Seaberg, has been singing with the chorus since his first week in Chicago in 1952. Yes, the chorus has meant a lot to Gösta and me. It still meets today at the Swedish American Museum.

Ja, the interesting people we met. There was always something happening at Verdandi!

Robert Altman
and *The Suitcase*

Having a restaurant in Chicago exposed us to some other interesting experiences.

The Swedish Consul General's office called us one day. "Ingrid. We wonder if you can do a favor for us. We have someone coming to Chicago who needs some Swedes to look like dock workers for a film they're making here. Can you help us find some?"

"Oh sure," I said. With our contacts that would be easy.

Film-maker Robert Altman and actor Carroll O'Connor were coming to make a TV pilot called *The Suitcase.* It was about a Swedish man, played by Gunnar Hellstrom (a famous Swedish actor at that time), who was supposed to get off the boat from Sweden with a bomb in his suitcase. They were going to film on the dock of Navy Pier and then at Swedish Covenant Hospital.

So I made some phone calls, and everybody I recruited got excited. We met at our restaurant one Friday afternoon and drove in a caravan downtown to the hotel, where our actors tried out for their parts. I got to stick around all week at Navy Pier and help by taking Social Security numbers and things like that. It was so much fun.

I thought it would be nice to have a reception for them at our

The film crew takes a break at Navy Pier. Robert Altman is in white (seated) and the main actor, Gunnar Hellstrom, is talking to him.

restaurant, so I invited them for Monday evening. I thought a few might come, but didn't expect that sixty people would show up. They must have liked our food because they arranged to come every night for dinner. They also had us make sandwiches for the entire crew that was filming at night at the hospital.

Robert Altman and his crew were making this pilot for a possible television series on CBS. We were all anxious to hear if it got chosen. The decision went down to the eleventh hour. But then Lucille Ball decided to stay on television for another season, so these two fellows, Robert Altman and Carroll O'Connor, lost their slot. We all know that they did pretty well anyway.

We really had a good time with the film people, and it was one of those things that you don't plan for but they just happen.

A Memorable
Visit to the White House

THERE WAS A PARADE on Clark Street in Andersonville. Our restaurant had been busy all day long. Just before closing, a couple came in, and I could tell right away that they weren't our regular customers.

They sat down and asked for *kroppkakor* (a kind of dumpling with salt pork, onion, and ham). A very typical Swedish dish, but we didn't have it. So English *sole au gratin* was what they ordered.

While I was talking to them, they asked why I had a photo of Senator Paul Douglas on the wall of the hall. I said it was because of Kiwanis, and that in our banquet room upstairs we hosted Kiwanis, Lions, Combined Insurance, and a lot of different groups on different days of the week.

When they were through eating, I said, "I would like to invite you up to the library and serve you Swedish punch and coffee." I realized they had come a long way, and I wanted to be extra nice. The man thought the punch was a little too sweet, so I said, "You can have *spetsa*." "What is that?" So I put a few drops of cognac on top.

We enjoyed a nice conversation, and then the man said, "My wife works next door to Senator Douglas."

I said, "In Washington, D.C."

"Yes." Then we started to talk about that. Before this couple,

Colonel Leonard and Hazel Bergstrom, left, they said, "You have to come and visit us." I was beginning to realize that people say that and don't always mean it, so I decided to see if I could make a definite date.

"Thank you, but when?" I asked.

"Well, when it's convenient for you."

"I'm going to New York in August."

"You can visit us on that trip, then. We'll show you around."

"Can I meet President Lyndon Johnson?"

"Now, you may be asking a little too much. I don't think so."

"Well, I'll be happy with Hubert Humphrey" (the vice-president).

One day I decided to call this woman, Mrs. Hazel Bergstrom who worked next to Senator Douglas. I learned later that she was actually director of the U.S. Employment Service for Capitol Hill.

Gösta was skeptical. "You don't know if she's from Washington; she might be from Texas. I don't think she's from the White House."

But I went to the telephone and asked for "the White House, please."

"Whom do you wish to speak to?"

"Mrs. Bergstrom."

"I don't see any Bergstrom here."

"Oh, yes, she is there, she told me that."

"There is no Bergstrom here." Then they more or less hung up on me. So I called back and got somebody else on the line and the same response, "There is no Mrs. Bergstrom here."

"Does it help if I tell you she works next door to Senator Douglas?"

"Oh, for goodness sake. You must mean Hazel Landstrom. She's married now, and we go by her old name. Just a minute, I'll get her on the line."

"Hello . . . . When are you coming?"

"I'm coming soon. On August 23rd."

"Then we will plan on that, and you can stay with us."

Unfortunately, they had a flood at their house, so I stayed at the Hilton Hotel. But I was there for three days, and those were the most wonderful days you can imagine. She would ask different people to take me around. She told the policemen, "If you see Ingrid around, leave her alone; she is my guest." There were trolley cars underneath the buildings that we traveled around on.

One woman took me to a restaurant for 11:00 o'clock coffee and then to the Senate Restaurant for lunch. She said, "You have to have the Senate apple pie. Nobody comes to this restaurant without having a piece of apple pie the first time."

When I came back, Hazel Bergstrom asked me, "So how did you like Liz Carpenter?"

"Oh, is that what her name is?"

"Yes, she is Ladybird Johnson's secretary."

"Well, she was nice, very nice."

That evening Robert McNamara, Secretary of Defense, invited us to a big reception for members of Congress and the Diplomatic Corps in honor of the three Colwell brothers and their large chorus of youth, who had just come home from a music tour of thirty-seven countries. They gave an exciting concert on the theme of breaking down barriers between people. After the concert the McNamaras invited a small party of us to go out for ice cream.

The next day we went to another good restaurant, and the waiters there knew Hazel Bergstrom, too. A three-piece orchestra played "Swedish Rhapsody" for us. We had such a nice evening, and we talked for a long time. Her husband's family had come from Eskilstuna, not too far from Dalarna.

The next morning I went on a White House tour. There was a line two blocks long to get in, but I was told to ask for a certain person, and then I was taken on a special tour for twenty-five people. After that I toured the FBI building, where they let me shoot and keep the target.

That afternoon Hazel Bergstrom went with me to visit

My visit with Vice-President Hubert H. Humphrey was an exciting part of my visit to Washington, D. C. I never would have had this chance if Hazel Bergstrom (right) and her husband hadn't happened to have dinner at our Verdandi Restaurant.

To Ingrid Bergstrom — with my warm regards and good wishes
Hubert H Humphrey

Hubert Humphrey. We heard that Lyndon Johnson was out of town, but we also heard that he had a bad cold and was in bed. To avoid the crowd waiting to see Mr. Humphrey, we went around the back way to his office. When it was our turn, we had to go in one step at time. One step back and forth, whatever the security people indicated with their hands.

When we got in, Humphrey greeted me like he knew me. He called me Ingrid and said he had a cousin or a sister named Ingrid. He asked, "What do you serve at your restaurant?"

I said, "Swedish beefsteak with onions!"

"Oh, that sounds so good. I'll be over soon!"

We talked some more and then he said, "Now we will call for a photographer to take our picture."

"Oh, that's all right, I brought my own camera." Hazel almost fainted. Since we had come in the back way, I had missed the signs that warned, "Photography absolutely forbidden."

"Let me see," Mr. Humphrey said. "That's the kind of camera my parents sold in their drugstore in South Dakota. It's a good one. But I think we'll have someone take a picture for us." He handed my camera back.

The photographer was there in two minutes. Then Mr. Humphrey said, "I'm going to send the photo to you." He also gave me a gold-trimmed card for the Vice-President's Gallery in the Senate Chamber and said I could come back as long as he was in office with that card. He gave me a book that he signed, a pen, and a gold dollar from the inauguration party.

"I'm going to send these things personally, and I'm going to jazz it up so you can show your friends. And your mailman will enjoy it too."

In less than two weeks, the package came, and the mailman exclaimed, "Guess who you have a package from?" The mailman liked that and had fun telling others about it.

I took this trip by myself because they had invited just me, and I enjoyed every minute of it. A local newspaper wrote about it when I came home. There were different reactions to my trip. "Don't they have anything else to do than to take care of you?" "I think you should take those pictures down." "I think you should really show off those pictures."

People were either for or against it all.

A 'Daughter' Margit
and a Little Friend Mary

DURING THESE YEARS there was another side to my life that was my private grief. I had been unable to have children. I cried every month. I went to a doctor and even went to the hospital for two days for observation. The only thing the doctor could tell me was, "If God wants you to have children, you will get them." I was very sad.

This feeling of wanting to have children stayed with us. One day we went to our pastor at Immanuel Lutheran Church and said, "What do you think? We would like to have an eight-year-old boy."

"Would that be wise?" he asked. "You have the Verdandi restaurant, and that takes all your time. You take a boy that age, and by the time you get him he's been in different places, and he would need a lot of attention. You would have to give up working. I suggest that you wait and see if there is a girl, sixteen or seventeen years old, more in line with your age, that you could take care of and feel that she was yours."

I said that we have had so many girls stay with us, and that's nice, but we would like someone who would be more a member of our family than someone who just comes to stay for a bit.

Then the minister said, "If God wants you to have someone, he is going to send you a girl, around seventeen years old, and she is going to say that she doesn't have a mother, and then you can be her mother!"

I thought to myself, "*Ja*, that's what you think."

This was a Sunday. On Tuesday, a woman named Berta Wesstrom from the South Side called me and said, "I remember when my niece stayed with you when she was here, and you were so nice and treated her so well."

Yes, that was Kristina Gustavson Gorne, who later became an opera singer in Stockholm.

"We have a girl here who came to stay with her uncle, but he is alone and can't keep her. And I'm having a hard time, too. You have a restaurant, and you don't have any children, so could she stay with you? *She is seventeen years old and lost her mother when she was thirteen years old.*"

I got chills. I could hardly believe what I was hearing because this is exactly what our pastor had said. I thought to myself, "God, how fast can you work?"

I said, "Can you both come here next Tuesday?"

They came. The first thing Gösta said was, "She looks like you, Ingrid." Then Berta and the girl went over and talked to Gösta. He didn't ask what her name was, how the trip was, or anything else. The only thing he said was, "When are you going to move *home*?"

We decided she would come and live with us after we got back from our vacation in the Black Hills of South Dakota.

I had an interesting experience on that trip. When we visited the Crazy Horse memorial, I bought a small replica of the Crazy Horse sculpture that was being carved on the mountaintop. I asked if the artist could autograph it.

"He's working on the mountain, and when he comes down for lunch he doesn't want to be disturbed."

"Well, just tell him hello from me, then," I said.

"And who should we tell him hello from?"

"Nobody," I answered.

A few minutes later, the clerk found me and said that the

Margit lived with us for six years and was like a daughter to us. Here she is as a Lucia, with a beautiful gown and real candles, of course.

sculptor, Korczak Ziolowski, wants to meet "Nobody." I was invited to the kitchen where he was eating a bowl of soup, and he asked if I would like to have a bowl with him. I declined because we were running out of time, and the soup didn't look that good to me. But he signed the replica, and we had a nice conversation. He seemed especially interested in the fact that I was from Sweden.

We returned to Chicago on August 7. We had said we'd be home around noon, but we actually got home about 1:00 o'clock, and the girl, Margit Ekstrom, came about 2:00. We have been very, very close ever since!

She is married now to Lars Lindblad, and he was Volvo's best salesman in America for years. They have a son, Charles, who recently received his master's degree from North Park University.

We are all as close as a family, and I have to say, we never had a harsh word with Margit in all the years we've known and loved her. Having her with us was very, very good.

At first we were sometimes a little silly, playing a game in public about being mother and daughter. We'd go shopping, and I'd say, "Oh, my child, look at that dress. Would you like to have it?" "Oh, yes, Mom, can I have it?" Margit would say. We were really fond of each other and enjoyed acting like mother and daughter.

I decided to take Margit to the southern sunshine during her first winter with us. I knew she would appreciate that because she had spent all her winters in dark Sweden. We went down in February, just before Valentine's Day.

One afternoon we went to the luxurious beachfront Fontainebleau Hotel in Miami Beach to see what it was like. We were in the elevator, talking and having a good time, in Swedish, of course. This caught the attention of a man who was on the elevator with us.

"Are you Miss Sweden?" he asked Margit. "No."

"But she has been a Lucia," I said.

"Would you be interested in being on the radio?" he asked after learning she was from Sweden. "I'm interviewing Jayne Mansfield this afternoon, and we'll put you on right after her."

"Why not?" So off we went. Jayne Mansfield (who was of the same era as Marilyn Monroe, and who could say who was more beautiful?) came to the interview on crutches since she had broken her leg.

The interview went well, and then the man treated us to dinner in payment for the interview. Later, this same man saw us in our hotel and asked if we'd like to go to a party. "It's Jackie Gleason's birthday, and he's having some people over."

We got to ride in this man's limousine and attend Gleason's party. I remember his beautiful house and the many people there. His birthday cake was heart-shaped since it was February. We left after a couple of hours. We didn't want to stay too long and get involved in anything that might be too much for us. We took a taxi back to our hotel, and looked at each other and wondered

Margit, Charles, and Lars Lindblad with Gösta and me at a recent Christmas get-together. The Lindblads live in Libertyville, Illinois. We are as close as a real family.

where we had been!

Margit lived with us for about six years. She was a joy, and it was so good to have her with us. She can be quiet at times and also funny at times. If I would tell her something that wasn't for others to hear, there isn't anything in the world that would make her tell.

She is a wonderful friend, and we see each other often.

I had another special friend, whom I called little Mary. When you live in a city such as Chicago, it's easy to stay in your immigrant groups and be helpful and sociable with other Swedes.

This is what happened with our little Mary. Mary's mother was Swedish, and her father was Greek. When the family was starting out, they didn't have much. So I would take Mary home with me for a few days at a time.

She was the cutest little girl. She was so fond of pink that everything I bought for her had to be pink. At our home she had her own closet with her little clothes in it and her own drawers with her hairbrush and pink rollers. I would like to have adopt-

"Little Mary," now grown up, spent a lot of time with us when she was young.

Mary's sister, Bessie, exhibited her art at the Swedish American Museum in 1990.

ed her after her family had three more children, but that didn't happen.

Even though this was more than forty years ago, we are still in contact. She lives in Greece now but visits us when she can. I don't think we'll ever forget each other. Her sister Bessie is a well-known artist living in Canada, and the two of them visit us occasionally. These two girls have been very important in my life. Their husbands work for the airlines, so they can get airplane tickets easily.

Maybe it's because I didn't have any children of my own and wanted some so badly that I've grown attached to Margit and Mary and Bessie and to so many other wonderful girls who have come my way. That must be true because I've certainly known and loved so many.

Mysterious Olle
and Friendly Stanley

LET ME TELL YOU about a very mysterious man. We first met Olof (Olle) Jonsson in the early 1960s when he was working in Chicago as an architect.

Olle was someone that a lot of people heard about and wanted to meet. He had a gift, maybe it was extra-sensory perception, but whatever it was, I saw it for myself. He could tell you facts that he had no reason to know, and he could even move things.

The first time I met Olle was at a dinner we had in our home for another couple and him. We were curious about what he could do. When everyone was seated around the dining room table, Olle asked me to take a piece of paper, write something on it, and seal it in an envelope.

I went to another room and wrote, "It was nice you came." Then I handed the sealed envelope to him.

Before he opened it, he said, "You should have said, 'It was nice that you came,' but you wrote, 'It was nice you came.'"

He was right!

Sometimes when people were relaxing around the table, he would all of a sudden read their mind. You never knew when he would do this. I remember once, when he was going to go somewhere with Margit, that he didn't really want to go with her because he perceived that she didn't think too highly of him.

I asked Margit about this, and she said that one time when she was sitting near him she was thinking that his cheeks looked like apples. I guess he didn't like that. He did have very round cheeks, red and healthy. But you didn't want to look at his eyes; they could almost see through you!

He would often come to our restaurant and have strawberry shortcake with whipped cream. We would sit and talk, and he'd tell us about his latest activities, which were always interesting.

Once when we were having a surprise birthday party for our friend, Hans Bjorklund, Olle asked if he could play a joke on him. Olle said he would make Hans' cake fork burning hot.

"Mysterious Olle" (left) with Glenn Ford, who was going to make a film about him. I don't think he did.

We set the table for about twenty people. As we started to enjoy the cake, Hans picked up a big forkful, put it in his mouth, and instantly threw the fork across the room. It burned his mouth, and he didn't think this was funny at all.

A few years later, Gösta lost his wallet. He usually kept it on the desk in his office at the restaurant. He knew he had left it there, and it was full of money. Lots of it.

We both looked and looked, and it was bothering us so much that we said, "Where is Olle Jonsson now?" But we hadn't seen him in a year and didn't have his address or telephone number.

Sunday came, and we were serving a big herring breakfast in the restaurant. We were still troubled that the wallet was missing, especially because we trusted everyone so much. And on this particular Sunday, Olle Jonsson walked through the door.

"Ingrid," he said, "what have you lost? Have you lost a dog?"

"Oh, I'm so glad to see you. Where do you live now?"

"I live in Kenosha" (an hour north of Chicago in Wisconsin).

"What are you doing here?"

"I had a feeling something was happening, and I wanted to know what it is."

We told him the story. He said, "I'm in a hurry now. I'm on the way downtown to meet Glenn Ford for a movie idea about my life. But I wanted to stop here and see what you need. I promise you that I will see that you get the money back."

Ja, but we have looked everywhere.

"Maybe someone who is walking around with it will be sorry and bring it back. I'll make him bring it back!"

"Is it a him?"

"Yes, it is. Gray hair," he said.

Just when he said that, I remembered an old man who worked for us. He had surprised me at Christmastime once by giving me a gift. It was a silver ladle exactly like one I had lost a long time before, a ladle I used for the punch bowl. All of a sudden I got one exactly like it from him. He said he had bought it second-hand. Who knows?

Now it was Monday morning, and the wallet was back. With all the money in it. Olle called and said, "How is everything?"

"*Ja,* the wallet is back," I said.

"But you'll find that there are ten dollars missing."

This was typical of Olle and what he could do. Do you know that the man we suspected, that old man, never again came back to our restaurant.

During this time, Margit lost an eighteen-karat gold bracelet that her father had given her. The sentimental value, as well as the dollar value, made her look for it again and again.

I told her to ask Olle, and she was hesitant but thought for the sake of the bracelet she would take her chances with him. She called him and described the bracelet. He was quiet for a minute and then said, "Look in the bookcase because I can smell leather."

She said, "I have looked in every corner. Everywhere."

"Well, look once more because I smell leather."

A year went by, and she forgot about it. She was going through her closet to sort out clothes she didn't want anymore. She grabbed a leather purse and threw it in a pile. Then she heard a clink-clink sound. What was that? Sure enough, inside the leather handbag was her bracelet!

Olle was here during the time that Robert Altman and Carroll O'Connor were in Chicago making the film pilot. We had a group of people over one night, and they all wanted to see Olle "do something."

Hans Conrad, one of the actors, said, "I don't believe in anything like this." Olle said, "Well, we can start by talking about that coin you have in your pocket, the one with a hole in it." Hans looked surprised, because he did have an old German coin that he used to carry on a chain. But he said either it was pure luck, or Olle had reached in his pocket without him knowing it.

Then Hans said, "Can you tell me anything about my home?"

After a few minutes, Olle said, "I don't know if you like antiques, but I can see two swords crisscrossed above a mantel, and they go back to 1700. If that is right, then I leave it up to you whether you want to believe me or not."

"I give up; that is correct," Hans said.

Another story. Olle was on the Clark Street streetcar with two friends. He said, "I'm going to stop the streetcar between Foster and Lawrence."

Wouldn't you know, the streetcar suddenly stopped. The driver tried to start it. Then he got out and looked at the car from the street. He was shaking his head and couldn't figure it out. Then Olle said, "Okay," and the streetcar started moving again.

This special gift came to Olle at an early age. When he was about five years old, he was sitting on the kitchen floor in his house in Sweden. All of a sudden he started to laugh. His mother said, "What's so funny, Olle?"

He said, "Hulda next door spilled milk all over the floor."

"How do you know?"

"I saw it," Olle said.

His mother went over to her neighbor, and she was wiping the floor because she had just spilled some milk.

The *National Enquirer* carried the following story about Olle. I know you can't always trust what you read there, but, knowing Olle, I believe this story.

A professional treasure hunter had the rights to search for the fortune from a Spanish fleet that sank in 1662. It was to be a group effort, with an agent from the state of Florida, the treasure hunter, his crew, and Olle.

They took off from the coast of Florida and went out forty-one miles. All of a sudden, Olle told them to stop. He stood up and asked three others to join him in a circle. After a few minutes, he said, "This is it. There is metal down there and lots more nearby."

He then went into a kind of trance and started to relive the night of the storm. "I hear terrible cries from the dying. I can see the water boiling in the angry storm. I see bright metal flashing past and landing on the shifting sand." As he was coming out of this trance, the engine on the boat sputtered and died. One of the divers said that this had never happened before. Olle said that strange things happen when he uses his powers.

The boat made its way back to Key West on one engine, and they waited a few days for the right conditions to return to the red buoy they had left behind. They went with a tugboat equipped with special pumps to dig giant holes in the sand. The divers went down and came up holding gold chains and coins.

These were priceless relics from the shipwrecks of the Atocha and the Santa Margarita, found fifty-four feet down. They carried a fortune in gold, silver bars, and coins. I wonder how much they found.

I don't want to give a bad impression here. I am a Christian person, so I know where the *real power* is from. All I can say is what I saw and heard about Olle.

Another unusual friend we had was Stanley Harzowski.

Was anyone willing to do cleaning jobs in the 1960s? Almost no one. We thought that, too, until we met Stanley, "Friendly Stanley," as Gösta used to call him.

Stanley was a veteran of World War II, single, and an alcoholic. So his life was a little different, but he was usually available for work.

Gösta and our long-time friend, Gunnar Seaberg, had become friends with him and found odd jobs for him to do. Gunnar let him sleep in the warehouse of his organ-rental business, so Stanley would have a dry roof over his head.

He was a lonely man, usually not interested in conversation. But when he was sober, he knew how to work. There wasn't anyone like him. He could clean, and he would clean, anything that needed it.

"Friendly Stanley" is at right on this Sweden Shop photo that also shows long-time employees Joyce Koza, second from left, and Britta Seaberg, second from right.

He would show up in the mornings before our restaurant opened and clean the tables. He would wash dishes for us if we were shorthanded. And he could fix almost anything. He told us about how he fixed automobiles when he was in the Army in France, and he was given a higher rank because of it.

After we sold the restaurant and bought the Sweden Shop, Stanley helped us with odd jobs there. He would come in early and vacuum and fix anything that needed fixing. He would go down the basement and clean. It never bothered him to do these things.

Gösta would pay him just enough to get by, because he knew that we wouldn't see him for days if we paid him too much.

We let him live in one of our apartments over the store when it seemed like that would be a good place for him. But one day the drinking got to be too much. The doctor said that he had more alcohol than blood in his veins, and if he wanted to live, he had to stop drinking.

Stanley decided from that day on to quit, and he did. Then Gösta and Gunnar looked after him. Every day they would take him to a Polish restaurant for his favorite food. He would order pork shank and sauerkraut. Good Polish food! They helped him become healthy again.

Stanley is living in a retirement home now. His Social Security and pension cover his expenses, and he has been sober ever since the day he said he was going to quit drinking. He comes to our home once in awhile for a visit and likes to see our cat Lucky. Lucky was a stray, too.

You know, Stanley had the keys to our business and could have taken advantage of us at any time. But he never did. He was one of the most honest men we have ever met. He and Gösta became very good friends, and the nickname "Friendly Stanley" described exactly what he was to us.

A Lost Passport

IN THE SUMMER OF 1966 we were taking a trip to Sweden. We had people who would look after the restaurant, and we were packed. Now we were at the airport with two hours to go before our plane would take off.

I looked at my passport and suddenly realized I had the wrong one. Of course I was told that I could not get on the plane. I had to go home and find the correct one. The young man who had driven us to the airport said, "I can take you home." Well, that was good, but he was new in this country and didn't know much about Chicago. I was sitting in the car with my head down, nervous because I was trying to think of where I would find my passport.

When I "woke up," so to speak, we were in Maywood quite far from the North Side of Chicago. When I finally got home, I knew I had missed the plane and I couldn't find my passport anywhere.

I called the airline, and they promised I could get a seat the next day, even though it was hard to get a ticket in the summertime. The plane had left with Gösta on it, and they promised to notify him.

The next day I still had not found my passport. I called the passport office and asked if I could travel without one. "No, you have to have a passport, and that might take a few days even if they rush it."

"In that case," I said, "I'll call Washington, because I have the vice-president's card to get in the gallery. Maybe they can help me get a passport today."

I really thought that might work, but the man I was talking to started to laugh.

But then he said, "If you really have that card, you can show it to us and we'll try to get you a passport so you can go today." I thought this is nice, now I can go. But I believe he thought I was just making this up.

"Look once more, especially in the drawers," he said.

So I looked again. Then I remembered that I sometimes used to put things under the drawer liner. I put my hand under the paper and felt something. There was my passport!

I called the passport office and told them I had found it. I also thanked them for promising me I would be able to get my passport and that I really did have that gallery card.

That afternoon I took off on the 5:00 p.m. flight. When I got to Copenhagen, Gösta was already in Malmö interviewing a chef for our restaurant, so I had some free time. I hired a taxi and asked the driver to show me around Copenhagen, since I had never been there before.

He spent an hour driving me all over, to the Little Mermaid, where he told me the story about the statue, and to some of the important buildings, churches, and gardens. I told him we had a chef from Denmark. After the tour was over, I asked him how much I owed. He said, "Eighteen *kronor*." That was not very much even back then. "But you have to promise me one thing."

"What is that?"

"You have to be nice to that Danish guy who works for you."

I said I would be extremely nice to him, and he said, "Goodbye and good luck."

I think the reason I was in trouble with my passport was because I've always had a tendency to hide things. Gösta used to say that we could never move because I wouldn't be able to find all the things I've hidden.

When I told him, "I don't think I have anything hidden anymore," he said, "Well, how about the necklace and the bracelet you can't find?" I can't answer that because I could have lost them or someone could have taken them. I don't know why I've had such a tendency to hide things.

My father was just the opposite. He left everything out in the open. When I'd go home for a vacation, I'd be reminded how safe it was in Sweden. He would say, "When you go out, just close the door."

A few years later it was, "When you go out, just hang the key on the hook next to the door."

And later it was, "When you go out, put the key under the rug." Different steps in security, because even in the small villages in Sweden nowadays, there are people who steal things, and it's like that all over the world.

Around the World in Three Exciting Months

AFTER OWNING THE VERDANDI RESTAURANT for seven years, we found that we were very tired. It wasn't an easy business, and there was always so much going on, so much noise, weddings almost every Saturday night, and so many details to take care of. It was either time to sell or take a break.

I had always promised Gösta a trip around the world for his fiftieth birthday, and that time was coming. We didn't sell the restaurant right away because the buyer didn't have the money. He managed it while we were gone.

But now we were going to go around the world! It was December 5, 1968. The last thing I did before we left was to go upstairs to the private dining room to say goodbye to W. Clement Stone. He was hosting a luncheon honoring Ann Landers, the popular advice columnist.

We flew first to Seattle and then to San Francisco for our flight to Hawaii. When we got off the plane I was waiting for someone to hang those Hawaiian flowers around our neck, but nothing happened. And it was raining. This wasn't the Hawaii we had heard about. When we got to our hotel, our room wasn't up to our expectations either.

When the rain stopped, we went for a walk. We met a couple who heard us speaking Swedish, and they asked, "Are you

Swedish?"

"Yes," we said and told them what we were doing.

"You should move over to our place. We are a group from Scandinavian Airlines here to celebrate Christmas in Hawaii."

We moved over there the same day and had a bedroom, living room, and kitchen, all for only $11.00 a day.

This group of about twelve to fourteen of us decided to get together and celebrate Christmas Eve at the Royal Hawaiian Hotel. We had a lovely time eating and dancing. One of the men asked me to dance and that was nice, until the next song came on and it was "Silent Night." I said, "Excuse me, but I won't dance to 'Silent Night,'" and sat down.

Next we exchanged gifts. Nothing was to cost more than fifty cents, and I remember that we all got something nice. I received four coasters, and I still have them. I bought a little wooden nut bowl with palms on it for someone else.

We spent every day with the SAS people and stayed there until the day after Christmas.

Next we flew to Tokyo, where we had a reservation at the Imperial Hotel. I had told Gösta we could stay at cheaper places later on, but I had to see the Imperial Hotel! I had also told my parents they could write to us there.

We showed up at the hotel and said, "We are wondering if there is a letter for Bergström? And we are late, so I suppose we have lost our room?" Of course, it was gone. When the young woman behind the desk handed me a letter from my mother, she said, "Are you Swedish?"

"Yes," we answered, and found out she was from Sweden. She explained in Swedish that our room was gone because the busy New Year's weekend was coming up.

I said, "You look so much like a favorite actress of mine who was popular when I was young."

"What was her name?"

"Inga Bodin Wetterlund."

"Oh, maybe that's because she's my mother!" She thought

that was such a coincidence. Somehow she found a room for us and said she would only charge us what she would pay for it.

She gave us a big beautiful room for the whole time for $12.00 a night. On New Year's Eve there were grand festivities going on. On our travel budget, we couldn't afford to go to those parties, but we walked around and watched the people in their beautiful evening clothes.

Charlotta, the girl behind the desk, was going skiing over New Year's weekend, so we didn't have much time to talk to her, but we did learn that her father had worked for ASEA in Sweden and then came to Tokyo and opened a machine company, and she decided to come and live with him.

A number of years later, when we owned the Sweden Shop, a Japanese man came into our store. He spoke Swedish as though he were born there, and we thought his appearance and his perfect Swedish didn't fit together.

I asked, "How come you can talk such good Swedish?"

"Well, I worked for many years at ASEA, now ABB in Västerås. When groups or the royal family come to Tokyo, I am their guide."

I then told him about Charlotta and our time at the Imperial Hotel in Tokyo.

He said, "Well, guess who got her the job?"

"*Ja,* who?"

"I did," he said. "It was a favor I did for her because her father was a friend of mine."

He then told us he wanted to spend the evening in one of the Swedish clubs in Chicago. Could we help him do that? I called Selma Jacobson, our "top lady" in the Swedish community in Chicago. I asked her if she'd like to have a blind date. She wondered who this Japanese man was and why he wanted to be around Swedes. But she said, "I don't have anything special to do, so tell him to meet me at the Swedish Club on LaSalle Street and I'll be there."

I heard later that they had a wonderful time, with many

We began our trip in Hawaii. It was beautiful after it stopped raining.

interests in common. When the man left Chicago, he said he was going to tell Charlotta that he had met me. I hope he did.

I have to tell a little story about Selma. She was so active with Swedes, both here and in Sweden. She once raised money so that a village in Lappland could have their own church. Before that they had to travel fifty miles to go to church.

Selma came in the back of our store fairly often to stop for a cup of coffee on her way to North Park College where she was working on developing the Swedish-American archives. One day she came dressed in her Swedish costume.

"Selma, where are you going today dressed like that?"

"I'm going to meet with Mayor Daley. He likes it when I wear my costume."

"Selma, do you think he'll notice that you have on one red shoe and one black shoe?" She was wearing Swedish clogs.

"Oh, he'll never know the difference!"

Through the years, we had a laugh over that many times, and she loved to hear me tell that story to other people. That was

Selma!

Our trip continued to Taipei and from Taipei to Hong Kong, and then to Singapore. In Singapore we happened to share a taxi with a bishop from Sweden. We were behind a truck with people singing and laughing, and there were people on the street dancing behind them. The bishop said this was a funeral procession and that the people do that to fool the devil, and they send the coffin on another truck another way.

In Singapore we stayed with the sister of our friend Ove Törnkvist, and it was nice to be in a home with someone who spoke Swedish.

It was always exciting to run into Swedes when we were traveling. This was 1969, and people didn't travel as much as they do today. We found that the farther we were from Sweden, the friendlier people were. If we heard Swedish spoken or thought someone looked Swedish, we would start a conversation. When we were in a hotel in Thailand, there were three of us in the dining room, and Gösta said, "I think that man is Swedish."

He was, and we spent a day traveling around with him and had a wonderful time. We also picked up two teachers from Perth, Australia, and the five of us became instant friends.

Next we flew to New Delhi, India, and then took another

We saw the beautiful Taj Mahal in moonlight and daylight.

plane to Agra. We arrived at the Taj Mahal in the moonlight. We had the good fortune to see this beautiful monument made of white marble in moonlight and daylight.

But in India it was sad to see so many children running around asking for money. If you give them something, you have a dozen or more running after you the whole time. I remember all the kids wanted to brush Gösta's shoes. He said, "We can't even go out for a walk."

I said, "You have sandals. They won't want to do sandals." And, sure enough, they looked at Gösta's feet and left us alone.

We next traveled to Tel Aviv, Israel, and it was the first time in fifty years that they had a snowstorm. We had to walk up to Mt. Sinai in the snow. We came during the time the Armenians had Christmas, about January 21.

I remember going to the place were Jesus was born and seeing many other places mentioned in the Bible. It's difficult to describe the feeling of being there. It is so holy because you know that Jesus walked that way with the cross and suffered there for us. And two thousand years later, we were walking in his footsteps.

It's also distracting to be there, thinking about the significance, when all around you people are selling things. You have to focus on where you are and what you're seeing and feeling.

Next we went to Madrid. It was spring there, and we could eat at an outdoor cafe. I went to a department store and bought a lovely coat, and I still have it in my closet.

Then on to the Canary Islands, where we stayed for two weeks. The first thing I noticed was a big sign, "*Det bästa med semester är att komma hem igen och äta falukorv.*" That means the best thing about a vacation is to come home again and eat *falukorv*, the special sausage that comes from Sweden. When you are lonesome for your own, it's good to come home and eat.

We had been gone a couple of months and had eaten all kinds of different foods. Now we could get the home-cooked kind of Swedish food, and we were so delighted to eat food that was familiar.

They had Swedish tourists in this place, and they had a few Swedish newspapers for sale. I hadn't read a Swedish paper for some time, and I was so disturbed by the tone of the writing. This was near the end of the 1960s, and Swedes weren't happy about the war in Viet Nam and had very strong opinions about that and my new country.

When we got to England a few weeks later, we were happy to be closer to home and to hear English again. And when we heard people speaking Swedish, we knew we would soon be back in Sweden. But when we approached these Swedes, they thought we were strange to be so friendly. They came to see London, and to see Swedes wasn't anything special to them.

After England, we traveled to France and Italy. It was very exciting to see the famous sights we had heard about for so many years. I think we saw every church, every temple, and every museum we could possibly see. Sometimes it was very tiring, but we had to do it. That's travel!

And then we went back to Sweden. We went to my home in Dalarna first, and that was wonderful. My family was so happy that we were home again after being so far away. We went to Lappland to visit Gösta's family as well, and they were thrilled to see us. We did some skiing, and then it was time to go home to Chicago.

We came back on March 19. We had enjoyed a long vacation, from December to March, with only two advance hotel reservations, one in Hawaii and one in Tokyo, and neither one had worked out exactly like we expected.

It was good to be home in Chicago again.

The Stock Market
and Other Ventures

WHEN WE RETURNED from our trip around the world, Gösta was doing a lot of investing in the stock market. I tried to learn, too, but I couldn't see that his stocks were going up, and I didn't have the patience that he did. I would say, "They're not going up. Why do you buy stocks that don't go up?"

"Well, you have to be sure you have a good stock. It doesn't have to go up so much, but you need to know that it gives a good income."

One day he got tired of my comments. He said, "Ingrid, if you think you are so good, why don't you buy your own stocks and see how easy it is."

"Okay," I said, "how much can I spend?"

"Well, you better not spend so much in the beginning. Buy a hundred shares and spend about $3,000.00."

Two minutes later I called our broker, Alice Blake. "I would like to buy some stocks that my husband wouldn't ever buy."

"Oh. . . ?"

"I have $3,000.00. I want a hundred shares, and I want something that is going up fast but that isn't going bankrupt tomorrow."

She said, "I think I have the right one for you, and Gösta would never buy it."

"That sounds good to me," I said. Then she mentioned something about "nursing." I was in a hurry because the lunch crowd was coming to our restaurant, and I had to be the hostess. "I'll take a hundred then."

So I told Gösta, "I am the owner of a hundred shares."

"How much?"

"Under $3,000.00. They were $27.00 each."

"Hmm, hmm, hmm. . . ." He's so nice he wouldn't say anything more than that. But this was his way of saying, "What you haven't got you can't use!"

"What stock did you buy? What is the name of it?"

"I don't know. I think it has something to do with landscaping because I heard the name 'nursing.'"

"That's something. *Ja,* now you will learn a lesson from this." Can't you just hear Gösta talking? Quiet and nice, still not exactly calm, but he left me alone as usual.

A couple of days later, I found out that it was a nursing home that was named Four Seasons. Well, that is an easy mistake, when you hear nursing, or nursery, and four seasons.

Then the stock started to go up, up, and up. Our friends on Clark Street knew all about it and started following it. Some days it would go up by five or ten dollars.

By this time, Gösta's investment club had started to buy it, too, and they were watching it carefully. They bought it when it was $57.00. I had already been through one stock split.

One day a friend of ours told us that the nursing home wasn't doing so well. Gösta said, "Now, Ingrid, it's time to sell. Be happy with what you get from it."

I respect Gösta's opinion. He knows what he's talking about, and I had been lucky. The investment club sold the stock, too, and a few months later, the nursing home went bankrupt.

But I ended up having the stock for a year and a half, and from my original investment I cleared $20,000.

Gösta said, "A blind hen can also find a corn!"

Now we were trying to sell the Verdandi Restaurant. It was

hard to get good employees in the 1960s, and we had to work so hard ourselves. We were tired from the long hours, and we thought there must be a better way to make a living.

We sold it to three doctors, and they had a man run it for them. It took us a few months to do this, and then we retired.

I will tell you what I did next.

When I was young in my home town in Sweden, I had to work a lot. I finished the "ground school" that all children take until they are about sixteen. In order to go to school at a higher level, called "gymnasium" in Sweden, I would have to take a bus to the next town, pay for the bus, pay to go to the school, and pay for the books. It wasn't like today in Sweden, when they even pay you to go to school. So I worked at home because my parents needed me. I never had as much education as I would have liked.

After we sold our restaurant, I thought I would like to sell real estate. I went to a real estate company and they told me I had to have a license for that.

"Ah, how do I take the license?"

"Well, can you prove that you have a high school diploma?"

I said, "No, I can't prove it. Is that what I need?"

"Yes."

"Okay, so then I will do that. . . ."

I started to study. Gösta said, "You know you're too old to learn." I was only fifty!

I would get up at 5:00 o'clock in the morning and study until 7:00 or 8:00 in the evening. I studied day and night from the end of January until March.

Then I went downtown to take the test, two days of testing, Thursday and Friday. Even Good Friday! I remember that there was a girl sitting next to me who was chewing gum and making popping sounds. That annoyed me, but I made it. Two days and eleven hours of tests, and I passed.

I don't know how I did it. There were all kinds of English literature questions, but if you think them through, if you have a little common sense, and if you've been traveling a bit, you can do it. You have four choices for each answer.

Next I had to take the real estate exam. The first time I missed, but the next time I passed. So now I had my real estate license.

I managed to find a job with a real estate company that was selling lots in another state. I soon realized that this company was crooked and was selling worthless lots. So I quit. I could tell this wasn't for me.

I guess I wasn't ready to stay home and take it easy because I ended up in business again. Gösta was working on our investments, and I got into the hanger business.

After our trip around the world, Scandinavian Airlines gave me a free ticket to Sweden. Whenever I went to Stockholm, I always had to go to NK, the big department store downtown. It is a wonderful store, and in their central atrium they are usually demonstrating something new. New clothes or new products.

The October day I was there they were selling hangers. Not ordinary hangers but plastic hangers that could pack down in a suitcase, then open up and become a form to hang a shirt on. Its unique design allowed air to flow around the fabric so it would dry fast without wrinkles. I was fascinated by the demonstration. It seemed like everyone who watched the demonstration ended up buying the hanger. I thought this might be something for me. I could do this!

The next day I went back and talked to the man who owned the business. He asked me some questions about who I was and why I lived in Chicago. And then I said that I came from Dalarna. He had been there quite often. "I have a brother who used to live in Södra Dalarna."

"He did. Where?"

He mentioned my village, Dala-Husby! It's not that big.

I said, "Can you tell me where in the village he lived?"

"There used to be a dairy farm, and that is where he lived."

"Well, that is where my home is."

We had lunch together and talked some more, and I said,

I am demonstrating the Dry-Ezy drip-dry hanger, another one of our business ventures. We sold millions of these hangers.

"Maybe you would sell this patent to me?" At first he said no, and I asked him again later on if he would think of doing that.

He sold the patent to us. I went home, and Gösta arranged to find a partner who would help us market these hangers. All of a sudden we had a machine and a plastics factory that made them.

We sold the hangers to catalog companies, and we sold millions. Whenever I went into a store to demonstrate them, I would sell every single one. But if I left to take a break, no one would buy them. They were difficult to sell without a demonstration, and the hangers were so inexpensive that it wasn't worth the cost of a demonstrator. But we sold millions anyway.

One time I was demonstrating them on the South Side in Chicago. There was a snowstorm, and it was impossible to get home to the North Side on a night like that. One of the ladies, a black woman, invited me to go home with her. I was so excited because this was new for me. I was usually around Swedish people.

We went to her lovely apartment and found that we needed to buy some groceries. We went to a mom-and-pop grocery store, where she introduced me all around. Then we went home and had a nice glass of wine and a good steak.

As I went to bed, I saw a picture on the wall of Jesus and the angels, and they were all black. Even though their color was different, I knew who they were. I woke up in the morning to the smell of frying bacon and eggs. That woman was very gracious to me, and I could get home after that.

When the tumble dryer came out, the need for a drip-dry hanger wasn't as great. Then someone stole the patent and started to make them in Hong Kong, but that business didn't last very long either.

One winter when I had some free time, I decided to try to learn French. I thought that would be fun, and I wanted to see if I could pick it up.

I liked learning the grammar. I thought it was like crossword puzzles, and I love them. But I had a hard time pronouncing French, especially certain words. Gösta teased, "You should learn English before you learn French!"

I don't think anyone would understand me if I tried to speak French, but when I try to read it I can get something out of it. And that's kind of an accomplishment.

The Sweden Shop—a Charming, Friendly Place

In 1970 the Sweden Shop on Foster Avenue was for sale. This was a charming Scandinavian import store in the North Park community that had been owned for several years by Myrtle and J. Irving Erickson. We would pass it all the time.

Now there was another owner, and he wanted to sell it. I asked Gösta if we could buy it. Gösta doesn't rush into anything. So he parked his car across the street from the store and just watched to see how much business they had, how many people went in and out. After watching it for awhile, he decided that there wasn't enough business and we shouldn't buy it.

But I had helped out there for a couple of days and loved it. I was 100 percent sure that this was the place for me! And now it wasn't going to happen.

So I came home and started to clean. I had plenty of time to clean since I had nothing else to do. As I was picking things up, I noticed a magazine from a church. I have a certain respect for papers from churches, and I had a chest where I put all the magazines and papers that I want to keep.

I picked up this magazine and noticed a picture of Jesus at the well. I looked at Jesus and said, "I am putting you in the chest, because the day I get my store, you will be my partner!"

More than a year passed. We drove by the store one day, and

Gösta said, "Oh, look, Ingrid, they broke your window!"

I said, "Don't say 'your window.' I can't have the store that I like so much, so don't call it my window."

"Well," he said, "If you really want it that much, call them tomorrow and see if it's still for sale. Then you can buy it." Maybe he thought it had been sold and he was saying that just to make me happy.

So I called, and it was still for sale. Of course, I went over there right away and discussed it with the owner. We bought it and took over on July 1, 1971.

On that first day of July, I flipped my calendar page over to the new month, and there was my partner! It was the same picture of Jesus at the well that I had made my vow to two years earlier. I realized that I had my partner in business, and now all would be well.

I went into the business feeling that nothing could go wrong, and it didn't. It was the best thing that ever happened to us. That store!

What an adventure this was! We had owned businesses but never a gift shop. Fortunately, we had great help to start us off. Brita Person, the woman who had worked there for several years,

The Sweden Shop when we bought it was on the south side of Foster Avenue.

stayed on to show me how things were done. Then Becky (Cedarleaf) Anderson stayed for awhile and taught me everything she knew. So I had the best beginning in the gift-store business that I could hope for.

My favorite part was the buying. Salesman would come in and show us samples, or we'd look in catalogs, and, do you know, I just knew when a particular item would be right for our store. I could *feel* it.

When the boxes would arrive, it was like Christmas! It was so much fun unwrapping the packages. Gösta would go crazy thinking I wasn't keeping track of what I was opening, but I was.

Some of the gift buying would take us to Sweden. We went to the factories and got to know so many people. One time we were at the Orrefors crystal company for a herring dinner. They sometimes use the hot ovens to cook herring and potatoes after the work day is over—an old tradition.

We sat at long tables, about twenty to a table. I happened to be sitting next to a Swede who wanted to know where I was from. I told him I was originally from Dalarna but that we now had a gift shop in America.

"What do you sell?" he asked.

"Oh, we sell lots of things, clogs, china, crystal, tablecloths, jewelry, and some food."

"What kind of food?" he wondered.

"Well, it's not a restaurant. But we sell lingonberries, and candy, and cookies. We sell *pepparkakor* (ginger cookies), but not just any *pepparkakor*. We sell Anna's Pepparkakor. They are the best, nothing else compares to them!"

He said, "Do you know who I am? Is that why you're talking about Anna's Pepparkakor?"

"No, who are you?" I asked.

"I'm the *owner* of Anna's Pepparkakor. And if you come out to my car, I'll give you some boxes tonight." We went to the parking lot, and he gave us many boxes of cookies.

This is what my life has been like. I open my mouth, not

knowing who I'm talking to, and it turns out to be such an interesting connection.

At first the Sweden Shop was located on the south side of Foster Avenue. It had only three rooms, very cozy and cute. We had so much merchandise that people would come in for a greeting card and stay much longer just to look around. We liked that, because later when they needed a gift or had some extra money, they'd come back and buy something they'd seen. It was as though family and friends were coming in all the time. We loved it.

We sold the best Scandinavian porcelain, full sets of china, and figurines. After the girls from North Park College became engaged, they would come in and register their "wish list" with us. We put a signature bow on all our packages, and since gift wrapping was standard for us, you could always tell which presents came from the Sweden Shop.

Bridal showers were always so much fun for the customers and us. Our shop was small and friendly, and we got to know the bride during her process of registering. I treated everyone who came in like I was honored that they chose our store, and I was.

When the women from the nearby North Park Covenant Church gave a bridal shower, many of them would come in, pay a few dollars, and sign their name to a card. I would pick gifts from the bride's wish list, wrap them, attach the card, and deliver them to the shower.

Once a year we'd have a sale. We would give 10 percent off on everything in the store, and we'd serve coffee and Princess Torte, the Swedish marzipan cake that is used for the most special occasions in Sweden. Many people had their first taste of Princess Torte in our store.

Our shop and merchandise were particularly popular because Scandinavian design was so current. All the Scandinavian countries were making products for the home, and we sold both the old-fashioned country style as well as the modern and fresh. We were able to show that you could have a mixing bowl that was both useful and beautiful and made out of the best materials. Even though these items cost a little more, people could appreciate the quality, and we made lifelong customers of Scandinavian products.

We loved pointing out the hand-painted china and how it takes 1,200 brush strokes to decorate one dinner plate of Blue Fluted by Royal Copenhagen. And we'd point out the artist's signature etched on the bottom of a crystal vase or painted on the bottom of a figurine. This never got old, because the merchandise was a form of art, and we were teaching appreciative people.

One of the most spectacular china patterns ever made in the world is Flora Danica by Royal Copenhagen. It was first intended for Empress Catherine the Great of Russia. It is one of the world's finest china patterns and one of the most expensive. It has a pink and light green coloring and hand-painted flowers on a white background. Every piece has a different flower. All the edges are scalloped, almost carved, and edged in eighteen-karat gold. Each one is numbered and signed. The artist writes the botanical names of the flowers in Latin on the underside of the plate.

There are three blue "waves" that are the mark of Royal Copenhagen china. They represent the three seas that surround Denmark. If there is a line going through the waves, you know it is a "second." Except for Flora Danica. There are no seconds. The Royal Copenhagen company sent us one of their artists to be in our store for two days. She demonstrated how the pieces are painted, and our customers really enjoyed this.

I heard recently that Oprah Winfrey has sixty place settings, plus extra pieces, of Flora Danica. I would like to see a table set with this. It must be more beautiful than the Nobel Prize dinner in Stockholm! Gösta bought me a cup and saucer for my birthday in 1973 and paid $250.00 for it. Today it would sell for $1,300.00.

We also sold a lot of merchandise from Norway. The Hearts and Pine Christmas pattern and the Farmer's Rose pattern of Porsgrund porcelain were especially popular. Because we sold so much merchandise from Norway, a man in Minnesota invited us to go to Norway with a few couples. A free trip for us in the middle of May!

Bergen was our first stop. Next we visited Telemark and then Porsgrund, where we met Grete Rønning, the artist behind Hearts and Pine. There we were also entertained by local folkdancers. Then on to Oslo, where we celebrated *Syttende Mai*, the national day May 17, and sang *"Ja, jeg elsker dette landet"* with the Norwegians. This was our first visit to Norway, a beautiful country we had heard so much about from our Norwegian friends.

We went through several trends at the Sweden Shop. One of them was the patriotic craze around 1976, the bicentennial year. All of a sudden Early American became very popular, and since it went well with Scandinavian products, we were excited about it too.

The Chinese laundry next to us was now vacant, so we cut through the wall and added another room. Now we had an Early American room. We sold so much Three Mountaineers merchandise, honey-colored pine shelves, candleholders, canisters, and bowls, whatever could be made out of wood. And we sold two kinds of American pewter that were also compatible with the old and new Scandinavian look.

One of the most enjoyable experiences of having the store was getting to know the girls who worked for us. Our super saleswoman, Britta Seaberg, was a friend from our early days here, as was Joy Koza. Joy was with us for ten years and was so helpful in the office. I can't think of those years without being grateful for them.

Most of the other help we had were girls from North Park College (now University). We just loved every one of them. Actually, we didn't hire that many different ones, because the ones we had stayed with us for so long.

Two Big Moves

IN 1976 WE MOVED into our first house. We had always lived in apartments. It took us all those years to decide to settle down in our own place.

We moved to our new house in March, and that year the lilacs were in bloom and other flowers came up by Easter. We hadn't asked the owners what kind of flowers they had when we bought the place, so it was exciting to see the different ones come up. We had both white and lavender lilacs. I remember a visitor from my home village came for Easter, and she said she couldn't wait to tell my mother that we had lilacs in bloom.

Our home is in Sauganash, on the far Northwest Side of Chicago. Homes were so in demand there that when a house was up for sale, a relative or friend would usually buy it. At the time we were looking, there were two houses for sale, and Gösta liked the one we bought so much. It is so quiet, and the neighborhood is so green, that it's almost like living in the country.

The area, named after Billy Caldwell (Chief Sauganash), also has an interesting history. In gratitude for his services, in 1828 the government gave him 1,600 acres along the North Branch of the Chicago River as a reserve. But because of all the new settlers arriving, he soon signed a treaty agreeing to lead his people west to Iowa. Charlie Johnson, a Swedish immigrant with money, bought 175 acres from the government in 1840 and began farming in what is now the Sauganash neighborhood.

This is our home in Sauganash, where we have spent 27 happy years. It is on the northwest side of Chicago.

When I heard about the Indians, I could imagine the Indian women by the river near our house, bending over to do their washing. Nearby on Rogers Avenue is a stone monument marking the Old Treaty Elm (which stood until 1933), underneath which the 1835 treaty was signed. This was on the old trail from Fort Dearborn to Lake Geneva. When our neighborhood was developed during the 1920s, this tree was at the center, and the new roads went out from it like spokes on a wheel. So this was real Indian country not so long ago.

The Sweden Shop also needed to move. We had been renting space from North Park College for years. When we heard that it had plans to tear down the building and build apartments and new storefronts, we wondered what we should do.

Philip Liljengren, a friend from North Park College and the neighborhood, happened to come in when we were talking about this. He told us that the building across the street was for sale, and why not buy that and move there? We were so thankful to him for telling us, and that's exactly what we did.

We now had to get the building cleaned out and ready for our customers. The basement was a mess beyond description. It was dirty, and there were dead creatures on the floor. Would we ever be ready and clean and comfortable?

But we worked very hard and got everything to look shiny and new. Now it was time for the carpet to be installed on the main floor. I had chosen a beautiful blue carpet with gold designs in it. It looked Swedish to me and was perfect for the store. I planned everything around this rug.

But now the carpet company couldn't find it. I called them up and said it was too late for us to select something else. You have to find it! I think I called them three times begging them to look for the carpet. But they couldn't find it, and they said the company in New York had stopped carrying it.

I called one more time and said, "Please, I have to have that carpet. Could you please go to your warehouse and look one more time?"

They called two hours later and said, "We found your rug, and we'll be over with it today!" They installed it that night.

This shows that you should not be quiet when you need something. You cannot give up! If I hadn't called that fourth time

Sweden Shop after we moved across the street.

we would have been in a mess. We had to move in, and we needed that carpet. Now we were ready to move on Memorial Day weekend.

One of the girls who worked for us at that time was Mary Hawkinson. She was a student who came in for a few hours at a time. Since we had to move the whole store across the street in one weekend, we needed all the help we could find.

Brita, Margit, Lars, some of our friends, a few customers, and some visitors from Småland were all planning on working with us.

So when Mary Hawkinson came to me and said she had a free ticket from her brother to go to California that weekend, I said, "Absolutely not."

She said, "But I have a free ticket, and I really want to go."

I was so insistent that she stay home and help us that I said, "Well, if you go, you can buy a one-way ticket, because you aren't

After we added the corner storefront, this became our Christmas room.

coming back here to work." Everyone else was sacrificing to help that weekend, and *something* was making me insist that she stay.

She wasn't very happy about it, but she stayed home and was ready to work.

On the Friday of our move, I was in the new store putting things on the glass shelves when Brita came in and said, "Ingrid, you need to come across the street right away."

I went over there, and when I saw Mary, I said, "I can see something has happened. What's wrong?"

Mary was as white as a ghost.

Brita said, "Ingrid, you know that plane that Mary was supposed to go on to Los Angeles? Well, it has just crashed, and all 275 people on board have died." That was May 25, 1979.

Even today I cry as I think of this story. Mary wouldn't be alive today if I hadn't insisted that she stay home and work.

Her father, Jim, came in and said, "Thank you for making Mary stay home this weekend." Then her mother, Alyce, came in and said, "Thank you for being so mean to Mary!"

After that whenever I left Mary in the store, I'd give her a long list of things to do, and she could choose among them. But she would always say, "First you save my life, and then you make me a slave."

Toward the end of our years with the Sweden Shop, we had

The owners of Nils Olsson Hemslöjd in Nusnäs, Sweden, demonstrated dala horse carving and painting.

a robbery. Brita and I were in the store on a Saturday afternoon around 4:00 o'clock. Two guys came in, and one was wearing a tee-shirt that said "University of Chicago." They were well-dressed, like two ordinary people coming in to do a little shopping.

One walked into another room to look at cards, and one stayed in the main room. Brita, who could sell anything to anyone, offered to help the man. He said he needed to buy a present for a diamond wedding anniversary. The other guy came in, and she showed them something appropriate and they agreed to buy it. They said they didn't have any money with them, but they would be back in an hour. "But I want to pick out a card," the one said.

The other one asked if he could use our phone. I didn't want him going into the little room where our phone was because our cash register was nearby. He said, "I'll go out and make my phone call, but can you give me change, four quarters?"

"Oh, sure," I said and opened the cash register.

Then the man came from the card room and suddenly pressed a small gun, a "Saturday night special," into my stomach. Brita had come into the room and said in Swedish that someone had found a toy gun. But I didn't have time to react to that, because I had a real gun at my stomach. The men took the money from the cash register and ran.

I went up on the stepladder and started to scream. It took forever for the police to come. They blamed it on the changeover to the 4:00 o'clock shift, but I thought that was a poor excuse.

I was very scared that evening. I was sitting in our basement, wondering if the robbers had our home address.

When the police arrested the men after another robbery, they had fifteen armed robberies behind them. They admitted they had been at the Sweden Shop, and they said I had screamed. I don't know why, but I know I did. Standing high up on the stepladder!

Most of the time we felt pretty safe at the store. I liked being in the community. In some ways it was like a small town. The small stores, North Park College, the North Park church, and Swedish Covenant Hospital were all within walking distance, and many of the employees lived in the neighborhood. So many people knew each other.

And so I always told the girls who worked for us that they should respect our customers and never talk about them. It soon got around that this was one of our rules, and people appreciated that. They knew they could come in and have privacy when they were in the store and confidentiality about what they were buying. It was nice for all of us.

In 1989, after owning the Sweden Shop for almost twenty years, we felt it was time to sell it. Gösta was in his seventies, and I was retirement age. Now we were ready to take life a little easier and think about what to do next.

We were happy when we found a suitable buyer. Susan Eriksson had experience in running a business, and she had the energy for the work, an appreciation for Scandinavian things, as well as connections in Sweden.

We still own the building, and we are happy that Susan and her husband and loyal employees are carrying on the tradition of operating a friendly Scandinavian shop in the North Park community. This year the Sweden Shop is fifty-five years old.

Nejmen, Vat Inna
Da Verld?

ONE NIGHT we got a call at our home at 1:00 a.m. The phone kept ringing and ringing, and finally we answered it. It was Charles, Margit's son. He said, "Something has happened here. Come as soon as you can!"

Charles lived in an apartment upstairs from the Sweden Shop. When we bought the building, it included four apartments on the second floor. Now we had to get dressed and go there in the middle of the night!

By the time we got there, the street was full of people and emergency vehicles, plus all of the residents of the building.

Someone had lost control of their car, and it crashed into the corner of our building. This corner supported the second floor in such a way that everyone was wondering if the building would collapse. What a mess it was, and in the middle of all the confusion, there were TV people with cameras trying to interview us.

The building didn't collapse, and the tenants all went back to their apartments. Eventually we got insurance money to cover the damage, and the building was repaired.

The car was badly damaged, and so was the building, but no one ever saw the driver. Whoever it was ran away, so we don't know if he or she was injured or if the person was ever tracked down.

I was upset about this at first, but Gösta with his calm personality made me feel better. I think people from the far north of Sweden have that quality. He is such a rock.

The experience made us so grateful for what we have, it really did.

A Little Red House
in Sweden

NOW THAT WE NO LONGER had the Sweden Shop, we
wondered what we should do next. Maybe we could get a place
in Sweden and spend summers with our families. What would it
be like to go home on weekends and see them? We haven't seen
them much since we've been in America. Now we have the time.
Could we have our own little place.

Of course, at first Gösta didn't think it was such a good idea.
He thought we could stay in hotels and then we wouldn't have
any worries.

A Swedish friend, Gunnar Melin, used to stay with us when
he was in Chicago. He was a baritone, and he would come here
and sing in various churches. He became a very good friend of
ours, and one day before he left he said, "Well, I have to go home
to Sweden and sell a summer place."

I said, "Oh, where is it?"

"In Dalarna."

"Oh, no," I said. "Where in Dalarna?"

He told us, "Dala-Järna."

He said, "It's so cheap that I've already told them once that
they should raise the price. I'll have to tell them once more."

"No, no, don't do that. What is the price?"

Impulsive as I am, I said I wanted to buy it. He said, "You'd better ask Gösta." When Gösta found out and realized I wanted it, he arranged with this man to save it until we came to Sweden that summer and could look at it.

When we saw it, we thought it would be wonderful to be so close to the woods, in such a beautiful house. It was painted *faluröd*, the dark red color with white trim that you see all over Sweden.

Inside it was kind of old-fashioned. The colors were like a Carl Larsson house, an orange-red and a medium green. It was a great combination of colors.

There was a white woodstove in the kitchen that we used almost every day we were there. Even though it was summer, the fire felt and sounded so good. That was my favorite part of the house. I would go out to the woodshed where I think we had a five-year supply of birch logs already cut and dried. The owner had left them for us.

So we would sit by the stove and read or do crossword puzzles, listen to the radio, or just enjoy the crackling sound of the fire.

Our little house was fully furnished. The couple selling it didn't have any children, so they sold it with everything in it. There were blankets on the second floor that still had the tags on them. It was very easy to move in. We didn't have any neighbors

We spent several happy summers in this red *stuga* in Dala-Järna.

The kitchen in our summer home was cozy, and we spent a lot of time by the fireplace there.

near us, so I could go out in the yard and sing or even walk nude if I wanted to! Only a few cows would look at me, that was all.

And the garden! Every few days I would pick a new bouquet of flowers for the kitchen table. I would put on my rubber boots and go for a walk and gather an armload of flowers. The grass was wet in the morning, and we could see those *spindelnät* (spider webs) and water pearls. And the fruit! We had so many blueberry plants, raspberries, and red, yellow, and black currants. If I wanted to find Gösta, and he wasn't on one of his long walks, I could go to the red currant bushes and find him eating berries. But I liked the black ones better.

We owned this house for five years. We were actually about sixty miles from my sister, brother, and father. So when we visited, we'd stay with them, and that was nice, too. We had an old Volvo that we kept in our garage. We paid for six months of insurance on it, and it would be waiting for us when we came back the next summer.

Sometimes we would go to local farm auctions where people were selling old things. We didn't need any more old things, but it was fun to go because it was like a folk festival. People served coffee and *korv* (sausage), and neighbors would come to see what people were selling. It was also fun to watch people try to outdo each other on the bidding, and they would sometimes end up

Gösta's mother in
Lycksele, Lappland.

paying twice as much as they would somewhere else. That was
what you did at auctions.

The people were unusually friendly in that village of Dala-
Järna, and this was a nice time for us. We had come from such a
busy life with so much responsibility and so many people around
that it was nice to come here and just relax. There were also nice
churches there. If we were in my home town, of course we'd go
to the church there, and there was one in Dala-Järna and several
in the surrounding areas.

My mother died in 1981, but my father lived until the winter of 2002. He was 102 when he died, and he was clear in his
mind until the end.

Modern advances in communication and travel were helpful
during the time my mother was very sick. When my family called
and said she was in the hospital, I flew to Sweden the next day.
On May 2 my brother picked me up at Arlanda Airport. I
remember there was snow on the ground, and this was May! On
the way home my brother said, "I have to warn you, Ingrid, I'm
not sure Mother will be alive when we get there. It might be too
late." So I prayed, "*Gud, hjälp mig*, God help me so I can see my
mother and talk to her."

When we got to her room, she sat up in bed and said, "*Ah, du
kommer, du kommer hem til mig* (Oh, you are coming home to me)."

I sat down and my mother started to talk. She was so peppy and wanted to know about Gösta and everything else in our lives. My sister whispered in my ear, "I'm almost embarrassed. I thought she was ready to die."

I stayed and visited with her until she died on May 13. I remember when I called Gösta to tell him the news, he said everyone was watching TV because someone tried to kill the Pope. *Ja,* that was the same day.

I stayed for the funeral. In America we have the funeral right away, but in Sweden it might be two or three weeks. I had to wait then, of course. But when I went back to Chicago, I was so thankful for the chance I had to talk to my mother before she died. She was so wonderful.

We sold our summer house in 1996. We loved it so much when we were there, but now we don't miss it at all. I suppose everything has its place in life, and when you are through with it, it's over.

Gösta was in the beginning stages of macular degeneration and had already started to lose his sight in one eye. Also, it was

My brother Erik and his son Mats.

becoming harder and harder to find someone to mow the lawn for us and look after the house in between our visits. We had already used my brother and nephews so much, and it was time they got some free time themselves.

We mentioned this to a Swede visiting Chicago, and he said, "I'll do it for you. Just give me the information, and I'll sell it."

He took down the information, and we hoped that he could sell it by springtime. On the coldest day of the winter in Sweden, on January 2, he called and said, "I sold the house today, to some

German people." All we had to do was sign our names a couple of times. Everything that was in the house went with it. A package deal.

I miss not seeing my family in Sweden, but I talk to my sister on the phone two or three times a week. She still lives in Dala-Husby, and her children and my sister-in-law's family all live in that area. They can e-mail messages and photos to us, so now we have to get a computer. I want to learn that next.

A Sad Time
on an Airplane

WE WERE GOING to Sweden for a summer visit, and so were Ulla and Folke. We knew them from the days when Ulla had worked for us at the Verdandi Restaurant for several years. Folke was eighty years old, and Ulla was sixty-five. Since his health wasn't so good, Ulla asked if they could travel with us to Sweden. Yes, of course.

As we were waiting in the lounge before our flight, Ulla whispered, "I think this is Folke's last trip to Sweden."

"No," I said, "don't say that."

We boarded the plane and found that we weren't sitting together, and we had asked to be together. That was the whole point. But we couldn't change our seats, so they sat on one side of the plane and we sat on the other side, but we could still see each other.

After awhile, Gösta noticed that Ulla kept getting up to go to the bathroom. "I wonder what's wrong with her," he said.

We were about an hour into the flight and started to have turbulence. I looked over at Ulla and made a praying gesture with my hands to let her know everything would be all right. Just then, Folke looks over at us and at Ulla. He calls the flight attendants. They call for a doctor and put Ulla on the floor.

"The life has gone out of Ulla," Folke said. They took her to another part of the plane, and Folke didn't like this. He said, "Don't take her away. She's my wife." It was awful. Now the plane had to land as soon as possible.

The closest airport was in Newfoundland, Canada. It was just a little hunting village, but it had a big airport left from the war when American planes would refuel there.

I got off the plane with Folke and Ulla, and Gösta went on to Stockholm.

The police had to take care of Folke and me. They searched my handbag and passport and said we couldn't leave until the next day. I called Ulla's sister and the Nelson Funeral Home in Chicago to make the necessary arrangements.

Folke and I were put in a hunters' motel for the night. I was supposed to be in a room close to Folke in case he got confused. But he could have been crying all night and I wouldn't have heard him. Those hunters were so loud and kept going back and forth in the hallway all night long.

We had a good breakfast in the morning, but Folke was still confused. We had to wait another day, and then we were allowed to go.

They put us on a cargo plane that had some space for passengers. At 5:00 a.m. we arrived in Montreal and then had to change planes again. Folke was so worried and wondered if Ulla was still with us. I stayed by the window to watch if they put her body on the plane.

Do you know, I will never forget this. I watched as four men brought her body to the plane. They walked slowly and reverently. They loaded her on and then bowed and backed away. I was so touched, and said, "Thank you, Canada," in a whisper. When we landed in Chicago, Ulla's sister and friends were there to meet us.

Later in the evening I went back to Sweden. SAS was so kind and gave me the best seat on the plane, right up in front. When I got off the plane, Gösta met me along with our friend, Gunnar Melin, the singer.

That's the sad story of my friend Ulla.

One More
Vacation Trip

MY MOTHER GAVE A PRESENT to Gösta once when she came to Chicago for my fiftieth birthday. It looked like a clock, and in the middle it asked the question: My wife is today? Then around the outside edge it had different answers: Friendly, In Love, Nasty, Nagging, Very Sweet, etc. You would take the pointer and put it at the answer you thought was right for that day.

My mother asked Gösta where he was going to put the pointer. Well, he said, "If I go by her moods, it would go around and around all the time."

She looked at me and wondered how it was for Gösta to live with someone like that. But he loves me and never complains. And he has said many times, "Why should I go to the movies? I live with Ingrid!"

Now I am much more calm and not so full of ideas as I was then. I think I would have made many mistakes if it weren't for Gösta. He would bring me down to reality at times. We're a good combination.

But after Gösta had lost his sight in one eye, I got still another idea. I thought we should take one more trip. We were expecting him to lose his sight in the other eye, too, but it hadn't happened yet.

So I asked if we could take a trip, just one more time. He wasn't so excited about the idea, but I said, "Let us travel once more together."

So then he asked me where I wanted to go, and I got my way. "Costa Rica!"

"Well, that is a good place. I would like to go there, too."

We bought our tickets and took the trip. One day we were driving up a mountain to see a coffee plantation that was just below a volcano. Higher and higher we went, and I couldn't take the height. I had to go to the back of the bus and throw a blanket over my head. But Gösta kept saying, "Oh, look, it's so beautiful. Look!"

As soon as we got to the top and got out of the bus, I was fine. The first thing we did was look at the orchids.

We watched as the people picked coffee beans from the bushes and put them in sacks and then onto a truck. The scale was on the truck, and they were paid right there for their work. They looked like naturally happy people and seemed to enjoy their work. I have good pictures of our time there, and Gösta has beautiful scenes in his memory.

At lunch they showed us how to make coffee in a ceramic filter cone. I bought one, and it's a good souvenir.

We drove up a mountain and visited this coffee farm.

We stayed in an elegant hotel, and their way of serving the customers seemed like it was from another era. In the little restaurant in the hotel, only men waited on us, and they all wore black tuxedo jackets. They served with a linen towel over their arm and were like a combination of maitre d' and butler. They treated us almost like we were royalty and were so polite and helpful.

We found that we were on the wrong side of the mountain for the sunshine and good weather, but we went into San Jose to see the sights and enjoyed watching the people. We were happy with our trip.

After a week we returned home. That was our last vacation together. Now Gösta wants to stay home because it's difficult for him to travel. I hope that one day he will change his mind and go with me. To Sweden anyway.

Two Questions—My Worst and My Best

I'VE BEEN ASKED if there's anything in my life that I've been embarrassed about, at least anything I'm willing to admit. I can't think of anything I regret, except maybe the time when Jim Thompson, the governor of Illinois, came into our store.

Jim Thompson had attended North Park Academy for high school, and his parents were good friends of the first owners of the Sweden Shop, Ruth and Hal DeGrasse. So when he was in high school, he spent a lot of time after school in the store. The DeGrasses' daughter, Joanna, married a Swede and lives in Dalarna.

Now he was our governor, and one day he decided to stop in and visit us after we had moved across the street to our new location.

I hadn't planned on working that day, but I came in to clean the basement. It needed it, and I was dressed to clean! I had found some dusty stainless steel trays in the basement, and I wanted to clean them up and put them on sale.

On one of my trips up the stairs, I stepped through the doorway and right into the arms of a big man! I looked up at him, not recognizing him, and then saw his bodyguards. Then I realized it was Governor "Big Jim" Thompson.

Flustered, I simply said, "Hi!" Then I realized how I must

look and that I hadn't treated him with enough respect. I was so embarrassed. I said I was so sorry but I was just cleaning downstairs.

"I look awful," I said.

"Well, I like people who like to work. So that's okay with me." He looked around. "Tell me where you got these white lilacs."

"I took them in early, before they bloomed."

"You mean to tell me they are from your yard?"

"Yes," I said, and we talked more about that. He stayed a long time and looked around the store.

"Oh, I see you have 'The Sandman' (a figurine). I have it in pink. It's an antique." I knew he enjoyed collecting antiques.

"Yes, I can believe that. I have the little statue of 'Don't Cry Over Spilled Milk' in pink."

"I don't have that," he said.

There was a girl in the store whose mother had gone to school with him. She went up to him and said, "My mother told me you were very shy."

"Well, you can tell your mother that Governor Thompson isn't shy anymore!"

Running into him was embarrassing for me, but he was gracious and didn't seem to notice.

Now the other question some people have asked is, "What are you most proud of?"

That is an easy one. I am happiest that I committed myself to God. I think this is the most important thing I have done.

I remember the date, the fourth of May in 1997. Six years ago as I write this. My life isn't different in terms of the way I live. I didn't go from bad to good. But knowing that I was forgiven was such a good feeling, and it took all my worries away. It was so peaceful. Whatever happens, I am sure about where I will go when I die. I was pretty sure before, but now I am certain! And so is Gösta. He has had a strong faith since he was a child.

Whenever I would get on an airplane, I would pray as we

flew. I would say in Swedish, "Please God, hold my hand, don't let go, and if something should happen, I will go straight up instead of straight down."

I feel that He is always holding my hand without my asking these days.

Spiritually, this is my answer to that question.

Businesswise, it would be owning the Sweden Shop.

Life Changes for Gösta and Me

GÖSTA LOST THE SIGHT in one of his eyes from macular degeneration in 1996. It is an eye disease that is somewhat common in older people. The center part of your vision is lost. You can see a little around the outside, or off to the sides, but you can't see straight ahead.

Gösta was so afraid when this happened. He would say, "What if this happens to my other eye?"

I would say, "Don't worry about it, don't worry. But we both knew that it could happen sometime."

Two years went by, and we had enjoyed being in Sweden for our summers. Everything was fine. He was happy because he could see with one eye. And if you know Gösta, you know he loves to read, especially the *Wall Street Journal* and other newspapers. Every day he needs to read those papers.

One Friday afternoon, I was baking cinnamon rolls in the kitchen. It was about 2:00 o'clock, and Gösta came downstairs because they smelled so good. He went and sat down in the living room, and then he cried out, "Ingrid. It's happened!"

I ran in there because of the frantic sound of his voice. He said, "It's blurry, I can't see anything." That was a very difficult, very scary moment.

"I can't see, Ingrid."

I called my friend, Stina Larson, and said, "Stina, can you hurry over here and take Gösta and me to the doctor? I'm so nervous I can't drive. Now he doesn't see anything in the other eye either."

She came over in a few minutes, and we took Gösta to the

Gösta enjoyed the attention of many friends at his eightieth birthday party.

doctor. A decision was made to operate on his eye. But the surgery didn't help. Then, of course, our whole life changed. One time he missed a step on the stairway in our home and fell down and broke his hip. Broke it straight off. Then he was in the hospital for awhile, and after that he had to learn to walk with a cane.

Life is very difficult when you can't see. You can't work and exercise very much when you can't see where you are going. But Gösta is doing very well with that. He takes walks on our street with his walker. Our little cat joins him on these walks. They go back and forth so he gets his exercise.

And he has had other problems lately, prostate cancer and lymph node cancer. He lost his hair from the chemotherapy, and some people thought he looked like Yul Brynner. But it came in again so white and wavy, and these days he looks so handsome.

But, *ja*, Gösta has had a hard time. But we are still so happily married. We get up when the *Wall Street Journal* comes to the house around 5:00 a.m. I read to him a bit, then we have some coffee and a little breakfast. Then we go back to bed and get up a couple of hours later and listen to some nice music. Then more reading and more eating. I like to cook for him, and he likes to eat. We also have our church and our faith, and we are happy people.

In the spring of 1998, we had a big party for Gösta's eightieth birthday. He was born on May 29, 1918. Our friend, Lennart Backstrom, a singer and retired professor of veterinary medicine, wrote a song about Gösta. "He's a Lapp without reindeer" the song said, mixing humor with praise. That was a happy occasion.

In Sweden on
September 11

I WAS IN SWEDEN in September of 2001. I was there to visit my father, who was 102, and I stayed with my sister Signe. We were having a wonderful time. Each day we had coffee in front of the TV. On this particular day, we heard that there was a special report coming up.

"Oh," Signe said. "Now they have too much water." There was a flood in Sundsvall, a town further north in Sweden. She was sure they were going to talk about the flood.

As I watched, I saw a plane going into the World Trade Center tower. And I said, "This must be a movie."

"The special is still coming on," Signe said.

But it wasn't a film. It was September 11. The planes hit, one after the other. I was shocked. I couldn't believe what I was seeing. I started to cry. They showed it over and over again.

And I know that I prayed to God to keep his hands over New York. I remember I said, "Please, God, let the eagle fly high in the sky over the United States." And then I started to cry again.

In the evening we saw how Swedes were lighting candles and putting flowers outside the American Embassy. People were coming together to cry and pray. I saw when the royal family of Sweden, all dressed in black, went to church to pray for America. I was glad that my home country cared that much for my new

I came home from Sweden after September 11 for our sixtieth wedding anniversary. Gösta made a wonderful speech at the party.

country.

After the planes were flying again, I had to get on one and go back home to Chicago. Back home to Chicago, to Gösta, and to making preparations for our sixtieth wedding anniversary. Life must go on.

A Very Special Gift

MY AUNT ALICE lived in Stockholm. We had always been very close, and I had sent her many things from America through the years. Now she wanted to give me something that I couldn't buy for myself.

A package for me came in the mail. It was soft and square.

"What could it be?" I wondered. Then came the story.

Alice's sister-in-law, Gärda Edin, had worked in the palace in Stockholm for thirty years as an upholsterer, the one who changed the fabric on the chairs.

One day Queen Louise asked Gärda if she would buy her a *trasmatta* (a simple woven rag rug) the next time she went home to Junsele.

Oh, yes, she would.

In return for this favor, the queen gave Gärda something from the palace that King Gustav V (who reigned from 1907 to 1950) himself had used. It was a cloth of beautifully woven brocade, about twenty inches square. It covered the table beside his bed. There were even two spots on it where he had spilled some coffee.

So Queen Louise gave this to Gärda. Gärda gave this to my Aunt Alice, and now Alice wanted to give it to me. Do I need to say that this made me very happy?

Some years later, after I had it framed under glass, I showed it to an historian in Chicago. He told me that it was very important to have the story written up and documented. I called my Aunt Alice and asked her to do this. At first she didn't think she could, but I convinced her to do it.

So I have a special tablecloth that was used in the castle in Stockholm by King Gustav V. And someday the Swedish American Museum will have it in its collection. Isn't that nice?

This brocade cloth from the bedroom of King Gustav V is one of our treasured belongings. Can you see the two spots where the king spilled coffee?

My Aunt Alice and I on our way to have lunch in the palace in Stockholm's Old Town at an earlier time.

35

Christmas in Sweden and Other Memories

CHRISTMAS IS A FAVORITE TIME OF YEAR for Swedes. When I was a little girl, my favorite time was Christmas Eve. That was when we opened our presents. Compared to nowadays, when children receive so many presents, we hardly got anything, but we thought it was wonderful. We might get some mittens, socks, a little candy, and maybe a little necklace, but no big packages.

And I liked the dinner because there was always a *smörgåsbord* with plenty to eat. There was a radio program that we would listen to that was special for that day. I liked the mood. It was so festive.

Then the next morning we got up early to go to church at 6:00 o'clock. We only had to go across the bridge, so for us it took only five minutes. But to hear the other people come with jingle bells on their sleighs, oh, that was beautiful. You could see the torches on the sleighs since it was still as black as night. These are memories from my earlier years, because later on people came in cars.

Something that still amazes me is that we had real candles on our Christmas tree. How could we do that and not burn the tree,

I asked my sister the last time I was home. She said we cut the tree in the woods only a few days before Christmas, and it was so fresh that it wouldn't burn. If you put a candle on a tree over here that was cut in September, it would burn right away.

I still put candles on my tree today. I have small tin candle-holders that clip on the tree. The candles are white or red and are a third of an inch wide. I don't light them of course, but I like the look.

So we would go to the early-morning *Julotta* service in my home church, which dates back to the 1200s. It's one of the oldest churches in Sweden. It is white with black doors and trim. It has beautiful windows, and the bell tower is over five stories high from the ground. The bells that ring on the Sabbath are so beautiful. I think they are from 1400 A.D., and you can hear them from a long way. They are a mixture of copper and brass, called *malm.*

During the daytime on Christmas Day, we sometimes had company for dinner, which was always special. If I got a doll, we would play with dolls all Christmas Day. I think I played with dolls until I was almost too old. I loved them. My mother would make doll clothes, and that was part of the fun. Having pretty clothes for our dolls! There was usually snow, and we loved to go out and play in the snow.

When I came to America, I missed my family at Christmastime. Otherwise we have had good Christmases here because we've had very good friends. In fact, for twenty-five years, we have been fortunate to spend Christmas Eve at the home of our friends, Berit and the late Gösta Gotstedt.

When we had the store, it would stay open until 3:00 or 4:00 o'clock on Christmas Eve. We were open from 9:00 a.m. to 9:00 p.m. every day in December except for Saturday and Sunday. So when Christmas Eve came, we were very tired. One time I even fell asleep at the dinner table on Christmas Eve. But still we would go to *Julotta* here in Chicago, too. That is something that is a must on Christmas!

The day after Christmas in Sweden is the holiday when you move around more and go to other parties. And since that was the day when we got married, we have something to celebrate.

Every Christmas I have to have saffron bread. My mother, who was a very good cook, used to bake that for Christmas. Whenever I smell saffron, I feel close to her. The aroma is unique; you don't find it in any other bread. When she was baking saffron bread, we knew Christmas was just around the corner. That bread was very special because we didn't have it any other time.

There's a little story from when I was in the first grade. I thought my mother was better than anyone else's. I was sure of it. One day my teacher was telling us that we needed to respect the Sabbath and not do any work on that day. She then said that if our mothers were really smart, they would make our Sunday dinner the day before.

Well, that started something. One boy raised his hand. *Fröken*, my mother makes our dinner on Saturday.

Another called out, "*Fröken*, my mother makes our Sunday dinner on Friday."

I couldn't stand this. I said, "*Fröken*, my mother makes our Sunday dinner on Thursday."

I went home and told my mother this because I was so proud of her. She said, "I don't do that." I said, "Well, I wanted you to be the best!" I always felt she was the best, and I said, "My mother says. . . ." very often.

We went to the Lutheran church on Sunday morning and to the Baptist church for Sunday school in the afternoon. And on Wednesdays they had a missionary for awhile in a chapel in Dala-Husby. This missionary told us that when we pray we should be on our knees. I didn't kneel. He then asked, "Ingrid, why don't you get down on your knees?"

"My mother said that these are new stockings and I shouldn't wear them out!"

He went and told my mother that, and she was so embarrassed. I don't know why I said that. I must have felt uncomfortable with kneeling.

Even though it may sound like I was a lot of trouble, I really wasn't. I was "something," but I wasn't trouble.

I was the middle child in a family where most of our clothes were homemade. So if something was store-bought it was really special. Once when my father came back from visiting his mother in Stockholm, he brought brand-new store-bought sweaters with buttons down the front for my sister and me.

When I went to school, I asked to be the one to tend the fire in the stove in the corner. The teacher suggested I take my sweater off because it was so hot over there. I didn't want to! I wanted to show off my new sweater. That was the reason I offered to take care of the fire and sit away from everyone else.

Another time I lost a button. I said, "I don't think I can go home until I've found my button. We have to go out and look for it."

I made the whole class go out and look for it, and they found it. My mother probably wouldn't have cared if I lost a button. But I was a good girl. I tried not to do anything wrong, but I think maybe my sister was even nicer.

Something that I've taken with me from childhood is my love of baking. I'm not that crazy about perfume, but I love the smell of baking bread. I also love to cook, and I don't think I can ever leave a recipe alone. I have to change it, add a little bit more of something. But to follow a recipe exactly is something I don't know how to do.

My mother would throw in a little of this and a handful of that, so maybe that is where I learned that. When we had our restaurant, that was different. Then we had to follow a recipe. But at home it's more like a game, and you can try to make something taste a little different.

Last Christmas I made some cookies for Larry and Patty at Tre Kronor Restaurant. They have hundreds of people going through their doors in December for their *smörgåsbord*, and I wanted to help them. So I made 400 cookies. They needed 4,000, so I made only 10 percent of them. That's not much. Next year I want to make more because I have just found a wonderful new recipe for *spritz*, a tasty Swedish butter cookie. That will be fun to do.

Write a Book?
What Next?

AROUND 1995 OR '96, I thought it might be fun to write a book. I was looking for something to do. People had said, "Ingrid, you should write a book." I thought they meant it, but people probably just say that if you've been around a bit and have had some interesting experiences.

But I took them seriously. "If you think so, maybe I will do that."

Then Gösta lost his sight, and I didn't want to do it anymore. I couldn't even laugh. It was a terrible time.

Then Channel 11, the public television station in Chicago, planned a documentary on the Swedes in Chicago as part of its Chicago Stories series. This series featured the history of Chicago and the different ethnic communities here. When it was time to develop the Swedish program, they talked to Larry, the owner of Tre Kronor Restaurant, and he told them about an older lady who would have a lot of things to tell. And their response was, "We have a lot of old ladies."

"Yes, but this one is different. She is young even if she is old!"

So I was interviewed by the producer, Risé Sanders-Weir, who came to my house with a photographer and asked me a lot of questions. They put the project together, and it went on television in March 2001. It was nicely done and was aired several times. Every time it came on I would get phone calls from people saying they saw me. I think I got 130 phone calls.

My interview for the series was quite long, but I was on for only three minutes. The producer chose to air the story about how I tried to get a job at the Hilton Hotel. So people were curious now. What did I do after that? It amazed me that people were so interested.

And then not long ago, my friends again said, "When are you going to get serious about writing a book?" So I started writing.

Then the Queen of Sweden came to Chicago, and at a reception for her at the Swedish American Museum, Kerstin Lane mentioned that I was writing a book.

"Oh, what about?" Queen Sylvia asked.

Queen Sylvia visited the Swedish American Museum and told me she wants to read my book. She really did say that.

"About my life in America."

"I would like to read that book. Where can I buy it?"

I told her I hadn't finished it yet.

"Promise me that I can have a copy of it!"

So when the queen wants to read it, what else could I do but keep on writing?

I wonder what is next for me at this age. I hope I remain in good health so that I can keep helping Gösta. Because we've always loved traveling, I would like for him to feel that he is traveling even though he is at home.

Now I hope that people reading my book will appreciate that this is the truth about my life. It hasn't been all good times, but that's the way life is.

And if some young people read this, I hope it will teach them not to be afraid to do things. The world is full of surprises and adventures. The opportunities are there, but you have to look for them and do something about them. Otherwise, it doesn't matter what the opportunities are. If you don't go after them, nothing will happen.

You know, if you have a car and no gasoline, what does it matter if you have a car? So you have to go and buy the gasoline! That's the key!

I Jesu namn

Till bords vi gå,

Välsigna Gud

Den mat vi få.

Amen.

My Favorite
Smörgåsbord Recipes

The *smörgåsbord* as we know it has existed in different forms since the sixteenth century. But it was not until the eighteenth century that it became very popular in Scandinavian homes. It was very convenient—just put everything on the table!

The word *smör* comes from the word for butter, *gås* means the clumps created while churning milk to make butter, and *bord* means table. The food of all Scandinavian countries is simple and down to earth. It has sprung out of nature itself and follows, to some degree, the seasons of the year. The soil, climate, lakes, and mountains all have harmony with nature and Scandinavian cuisine.

Following are some of my favorite recipes for a traditional *smörgåsbord*. Enjoy!

I'm putting the final touches on our Christmas *smörgåsbord* at the Verdandi Restaurant. *Ja*, it was hard work, but so much fun to serve.

Traditional Smörgåsbord Dishes

Westcoast Salad (Västkustsallad)

This unusual and delicious salad is named for the Swedish West Coast, which is famous for its variety of good fresh seafood. There is nothing set about this recipe; you can easily add or deduct ingredients to your taste. In Sweden this salad is served as an appetizer with toasted bread and butter. It is an attractive way to start a dinner.

1 1/2 cups crabmeat, drained
1 lb. shrimp, boiled, chilled, and drained
1/2 lb. lobster, boiled, chilled, and drained (optional)
1/2 lb. mushrooms, cut in slices
2 tomatoes, cut in thin wedges
1 cup asparagus tips, lightly steamed, drained, chopped
1/4 cup celery, sliced
1 head of lettuce, finely sliced

DRESSING:
1/2 cup salad oil
1/4 cup wine vinegar
Dash of salt
Dash of freshly ground white pepper
Pinch of garlic powder (optional)
1 teaspoon dark French mustard
2 tablespoons finely chopped dill sprigs

ALTERNATE DRESSING:
1/2 cup whipped heavy cream
1/2 cup mayonnaise
1 tablespoon chili sauce
1 tablespoon sweet pickle relish
Dash of salt
Dash of white pepper
2 tablespoons finely chopped fresh dill (optional)

Mix together all ingredients and chill. Just before serving, turn salad onto a bed of crisp finely sliced lettuce. Top with dressing.

Herring Salad (Sillsallad)

1 cup matjes or pickled herring, chopped
1/2 lb. veal or beef, cooked and chopped
1/2 cup potatoes, boiled, chilled, and chopped
3 cups beets (canned or cooked), chilled and chopped
1/2 cup apples, diced
1/3 cup dill pickles, diced
1/3 cup onion, diced
A bit of finely chopped dill
2 tablespoons wine vinegar
Dash of salt and black pepper
3 hard-boiled eggs
1 tablespoon mustard
2 tablespoons vinegar
1/4 cup oil
4 tablespoons heavy cream
1 cup sour cream
3 tablespoons beet juice
1 teaspoon lemon juice

In a large bowl, mix herring, meat, potatoes, beets, apples, onions, and pickles. Take the tablespoons of vinegar and mix in dill; add salt and pepper to taste. Pour over the salad ingredients and toss gently with a wooden spoon.

Remove the yolks from the hard-boiled eggs. Mince the whites and set them aside. Mash the yolks into a paste with the tablespoon of mustard. Gradually beat in the vinegar and oil, then add the sour cream and juices until it thickens like heavy cream. Pour over the salad, toss, and chill for a few hours.

Pickled Herring

4-5 herring fillets
2 large red onions, sliced
2/3 cup white vinegar
2/3 cup water
1 cup sugar
10 whole allspice

Slice fillets diagonally into one-inch pieces. Soak in water and cover for 12 hours. Drain. Boil vinegar, sugar, and allspice together. Alternate red onion and fillets. Pour vinegar solution to cover.

The herring will keep in the refrigerator for at least one week.

Matjes Herring with Sour Cream

Matjes Herring with Sour Cream can be bought in most Scandinavian food stores ready to serve. However, the addition of fresh chives is almost a must-have. If it is hard to find chives, leeks can be used instead. Mix with the prepared herring. Serve with hot boiled potatoes.

Krydd-sill

4 herring fillets, uncooked and cut in one-inch pieces
1/2 tablespoon black pepper
1/2 tablespoon mustard seeds
1/2 tablespoon juniper
1/2 tablespoon dill seeds
1 bay leaf
1 small leek
1/2 cup chopped dill

Soak herring in water for 12-14 hours.

MIX TOGETHER AND POUR OVER HERRING:
1/4 cup vinegar
1 cup water
1 cup sugar

Crêpes HKH

See Crêpes Suzette for crêpe recipe.

FILLING:
1 pound shrimp
2 egg yolks
2/3 cup melted butter
3 teaspoons fresh lemon juice
3-4 tablespoons dill, finely chopped

Place the egg yolks in the top of a double boiler and heat over warm water. Slowly add the melted butter, beat until the sauce is thick and shiny. Stir in the well-drained shrimp (cut into smaller pieces if necessary). Add the dill.

Place a little of the filling on each crêpe. Roll together and place seam-side down in a greased ovenproof dish. Sprinkle with grated cheese and bake at 435 degrees for 6-7 minutes. Serve at once.

Jansson's Temptation

This is supposedly named after Erik Jansson, the nineteenth-century religious zealot and self-appointed prophet who founded a colony with his disciples in Bishop Hill, Illinois. He preached adamantly against the pleasures of the flesh, but one day, it is said, he was sorely tempted by this dish. As the story goes, he threw out his convictions and ate it in secret, of course, but he was caught in the act by a follower, which just goes to show what this dish can do to a Swede.

6 large potatoes cut julienne-style (submerse in cold water to prevent browning)
1 cup heavy cream
15 anchovy fillets (reserve the liquid)
4 medium sliced onions
White pepper to taste

Sauté onions in butter, stirring frequently until golden brown. Grease a medium-deep casserole dish that is oven safe. Drain potatoes and dry with paper towel. Place half of the potatoes on bottom of the dish, followed by the anchovies and onions. Top with potatoes and sprinkle with pepper. Pour anchovy liquid over potatoes. Pour 1/2 cup cream over potatoes. Bake at 400 degrees for 15 minutes; then pour the rest of the cream over the potatoes and bake for an additional 25-35 minutes, until potatoes are cooked through.

Poached Salmon

Boil salmon in a fish pot with about 3 quarts of water, 2 1/2 tablespoons salt, and a few drops of lemon juice.

Pickled Beets

This dish should never be missing on a Scandinavian smörgåsbord.

Scrub, rinse, and cook a couple of pounds of whole beets in water with no salt. When the beets are half soft, pour out cooking water and chill under running cold water. Add the following mixture:

3 cups white vinegar
3/4 - 1 cup sugar
5 whole cloves
3 allspice
1 small bay leaf (optional)

Chill for several hours before serving.

Boiled Beef (Pepparrotskött)

3-4 lb. beef chuck with bone
1 1/2 quarts water
2 1/2 teaspoons salt
1 onion, cut in chunks
2 carrots, cut in pieces
2 stalks celery, cut in pieces

SAUCE:
2 tablespoons butter or margarine
2 tablespoons flour
1 cup beef liquid
1 cup milk
3-4 teaspoons grated horseradish

Place meat in heavy saucepan and cover with water. Add salt and onions. Bring to a boil. Reduce heat and simmer for an hour. Add the rest of the vegetables and cook for another 45-60 minutes.

Remove meat and vegetables and keep them warm. Skim the fat off the remaining liquid. Reserve one cup beef liquid. Melt butter and stir flour into it, then add gradually milk and horseradish.

Serve with potatoes and the vegetables.

Lutfisk

You can buy lutfisk in a local Swedish store or frozen in 1 1/2 lb. bags from IKEA (Viking brand). In a microwave-safe bowl, cover the bottom with 1 tablespoon salt, then arrange lutfisk, skin down, in the bowl. Add another tablespoon of salt on top of lutfisk and microwave for 15 minutes. Check. Most likely you'll need to cook for an additional 3-4 minutes, depending on the power of your microwave.

SAUCE:
3 teaspoons butter
2 tablespoons flour
1 1/2 to 2 cups half-and-half or milk
1/8 teaspoon salt
Pinch white pepper
Add a touch of mustard or sugar if you like

Melt butter and stir in flour until well blended. Stir in milk and cook, stirring until thickened. Add salt and pepper.

Serve fish with sauce over it and sprinkle crushed allspice on top.

Salmon Marinated in Dill (Gravlax)

3 lbs. fresh salmon (center cut)
1 large bunch dill
1/4 cup salt or sea salt
1/4 cup sugar
3 tablespoons crushed white pepper

Ask the fish dealer to cut the salmon in half lengthwise and remove the backbone. Place half the fish, skin down, in a deep baking dish. Put fresh dill under and on top of the fish. Mix salt, sugar, and pepper and sprinkle over the fish. Top with the other half of the fish, skin upwards. Cover the fish with aluminum foil and place something heavy on top for pressure. After 20 hours turn the fish over and press for another 20 hours.

When your gravlax is finished, remove from dish and pat dry. Scrape away the dill. Place the separated halves, skin-side down, on a carving board and slice thinly on a diagonal, detaching each slice from the skin.

GRAVLAX SAUCE:
3 tablespoons prepared European mustard
1 tablespoon sugar
1 tablespoon vinegar
1 egg yolk, optional
1/2 teaspoon salt
Dash of white pepper
1/2 cup vegetable oil
2 tablespoons finely chopped dill

Mix mustard, sugar, vinegar, egg yolk, salt, and pepper. Pour oil slowly over mixture and stir. Add dill.

Brown Beans (Bruna Bönor)

A favorite of Greta Garbo.

2 cups brown beans (preferably Swedish)
6 cups water
1 1/4 teaspoon salt
1/2 cup brown sugar
3-4 tablespoons dark corn syrup
1/4 cup vinegar
1 stick cinnamon (optional)

Rinse beans and place in a large pot and cover with water. Let stand overnight. Bring the water and beans to a boil over medium heat—add more water if necessary. Add salt. Cover beans and simmer for 1 1/2 hours or more, until tender. Add corn syrup, brown sugar, and cinnamon, and simmer another 30 minutes until thick. Season with additional salt, vinegar, and syrup, if desired.

Rice á la Malta

2/3 cup rice
2 tablespoons sugar
2 tablespoons vanilla sugar
1 cup heavy whipping cream

Boil rice according to package directions. Rinse with cold water and drain well. Beat the cream until thick and flavor with vanilla sugar and additional sugar. Blend the rice into the cream mixture. Serve with fruit sauce, Melba sauce, or berry preserves.

Christmas Ham I (Julskinka)

10-15 lb. salted ham (bone-in or boneless)
2 eggs
3-4 tablespoons mustard
1 tablespoon sugar
3-4 tablespoons dried bread crumbs

Quickly rinse the ham in cold water and wrap in aluminum foil. Insert meat thermometer into thickest part of the ham. Place on a rack in roasting pan and bake at 400 degrees until thermometer reads 165 degrees. Allow 25-30 minutes per pound.

Remove ham from the oven and loosen the rind. Place the ham on a rack in the roasting pan. Mix together the egg, mustard, and sugar to make a glaze. Coat the ham with the glaze and sprinkle bread crumbs on top. Return to the oven and bake until golden brown.

Christmas Ham II (Julskinka)

I get nostalgic over this recipe. Just reading the instructions makes me wish for Christmastimes past.

10 lb. salted ham (bone-in or boneless)
5 peppercorns
1 bay leaf
1 carrot
1 small yellow onion

Place ham in a casserole dish with the skin up. Cover with water. Bring water to a boil and cook for 30 minutes per pound. Skim off the fat. Add carrot and onion. Simmer until tender. Remove skin while the ham is still warm.

GLAZE:
1 egg
2 tablespoons mustard
1 tablespoon sugar
2 tablespoons bread crumbs

Mix first three ingredients together and spread over ham. Then pat bread crumbs over ham. Bake at 450 degrees for about 10 minutes or until golden brown.

Swedish Meatballs (Köttbullar)

1 lb. ground beef
3 oz. ground pork
2 tablespoons grated or chopped onion
1 egg
2 tablespoons bread crumbs
1 tablespoon potato flour or cornstarch or one boiled potato
1 teaspoon salt
Dash of white or black pepper
4 tablespoons butter

Mix all ingredients and work into a smooth texture. Add a splash of milk if necessary. Shape into small balls (about 1" in diameter) and fry in lightly browned butter for 3-5 minutes. Shake pan often to prevent meatballs from sticking.

GRAVY:
Add 1/2 cup beef bouillon to the meat juice left in the pans. Add one cup heavy cream, and blend in 3 tablespoons of flour. Bring to a boil, stirring constantly, to thicken.

Fish Gratin Deluxe (Fiskgratin)

3 lb. filleted fish (orange roughy, turbot, or sole)
1 1/2 cups boiling water
1 tablespoon salt
1 small onion, chopped
Dill
Parsley
3-4 whole white peppercorns

FILLING:
1/2 lb. boiled lobster (or canned), or shrimp
1/4 lb. sautéed mushrooms or truffles

SAUCE:
2 tablespoons butter or margarine
3 tablespoons flour
1 cup fish stock (water from start)
1 cup cream
2 egg yolks
Dash salt

2 tablespoons Parmesan cheese

Mix water, salt, onion, dill, parsley, and peppercorn. Boil for ten minutes.
Put fish on rack in a pan; fill the pan with the boiled mixture to nearly the
bottom of the fish. Simmer water under the fish for 10 minutes.

Put fish fillets in a greased oven-safe dish. Mix filling, divide and spread on
fish.

SAUCE:
Brown the butter and flour, add liquid, cook for 3-5 minutes. Remove
sauce from heat, stir in egg yolks, add a little butter, season to taste.
Cover fish with sauce and cook at 400 degrees for 10-15 minutes. Sprinkle
Parmesan cheese on the fish and cook for an additional 10 minutes.

Gösta's Glögg

A must-have for Christmastime. This is the same glögg we gave to Mayor Richard J. Daley for a Christmas present.

1 gallon port wine
3 cups claret wine
1 1/2 cups brandy
1 lb. sugar
1 package glögg spices. (Use only 4-5 cloves. If there are more cloves, take them out.)

Put glögg spices in a cheesecloth bag and into a large kettle. Then pour in the wines and bring it to a slow boil for a few minutes.

Put the sugar in a separate pot with a little water, melt it down, and then let it burn to a brown color, stirring constantly.

Next pour the sugar and brandy into the large kettle. Stir until mixed. Take a match and light the top of the liquid. Let it burn for one minute. Turn off heat and cover the kettle. Let it sit until cool. Pour into bottles.

Desserts

Raspberry Jelly Roll (Rulltårta)

3 eggs
3/4 cup sugar
1 cup sifted all-purpose flour
1 teaspoon baking powder
1/3 cup water
1 teaspoon vanilla extract
Raspberry preserves for filling

Preheat oven to 375 degrees. Line a sheet cake pan (15 x 10 inches) with buttered wax paper. Beat the eggs until foamy, gradually add sugar and beat until thick and lemon colored. Sift flour and baking powder together, gradually add flour mixture alternately with the water and vanilla. Spread the batter in the pan. Bake for 5 minutes or until golden. Sprinkle the cake with powdered sugar and turn upside down on wax paper. Spread raspberry preserves over the cake. Roll it up from the 10-inch side. Slice and serve.

Crêpes Suzette

This is the story as I have always heard it. Edward VII of England was known to love good food; he was also known for his love of elegant and sophisticated ladies. The story says that the king, in 1896, dined in Monte Carlo, where he was served a dessert of small thin pancakes, crêpes, with orange sauce. Someone spilled cognac on the pancakes. Another person thought to put a match to it and flambé it. The king loved it and decided to call it after one of the ladies at the table, Suzette.

CRÊPES:
1 cup all-purpose flour
1/4 teaspoon salt
1 1/4 cups milk
2 eggs
2 tablespoons butter or margarine, melted
Vegetable oil

SAUCE:
2 tablespoons butter
1/4 cup powdered sugar
Juice from one orange
1/4 cup Grand Marnier, cognac, or brandy
2 oranges, peeled and sectioned

PRESENTATION:
3 tablespoons Grand Marnier, cognac, or brandy

Combine flour, salt, and cream, beating at medium speed until smooth. Add eggs and beat well; stir in melted butter. Refrigerate batter for one hour. (This allows the flour particles to swell and soften so crêpes will be light in texture.)

Brush bottom of a 6-inch crêpe pan or heavy skillet lightly with oil; place crêpe pan over medium heat until just hot, but not smoking. Pour 2 tablespoons of batter onto pan, then quickly tilt it in all directions until batter covers pan with a thin film. Cook about one minute. Lift edge of crêpe to test for doneness. Crêpe is ready for flipping when it can be shaken loose from pan. Flip and cook for an additional 30 seconds. Place crêpes on a towel and allow to cool. Store crêpes stacked between layers of waxed paper to prevent sticking.

Mix sauce ingredients together, cook over low heat for 10 minutes, stirring frequently. Add oranges and liqueur. Keep warm. Spoon half the sauce into the bottom of an oven-safe dish. Pour a tablespoon of sauce over each crêpe then fold it in half and then into a quarter. Place crêpes in the sauce; when done cover the crêpes with the remaining sauce.

Place liqueur in a small, long-handled saucepan, heat just until warm (do not boil). Pour over crêpes and ignite with a long match. After flames die down, serve crêpes immediately.

Peach Melba

Nellie Melba was an Australian opera singer. At the end of the 1800s she took Europe by storm. Famed Chef August Escoffier of the Savoy Hotel in London created this dessert for her. She liked it so much that she gave him permission to call it Peach Melba.

RASPBERRY SAUCE:
1 cup frozen raspberries, thawed
1 teaspoon sugar
1 teaspoon cornstarch

PEACH PREPARATION:
3 cups water
1 cup sugar
1 teaspoon lemon zest
1 teaspoon vanilla extract
2 fresh peaches (or four canned halves)

PRESENTATION:
4 cups vanilla ice cream
1/2 cup whipped cream

Combine raspberries, 1 teaspoon sugar, and cornstarch in a small saucepan. Cook over low heat until thickened, about 10 minutes. Strain through a fine sieve; cool.

Heat 1 cup sugar, water, lemon peel, and vanilla in a large saucepan over low heat until sugar dissolves, about 5 minutes. Add peaches; cook until tender, about 10 minutes. Refrigerate until chilled. Drain peaches. If fresh peaches are used, then peel, cut into halves from top to bottom and discard pits. Place a peach half in each dessert dish. Place 1 cup of ice cream on top of each peach half. Drizzle sauce over ice cream. Garnish with whipped cream. Serve immediately.

Pineapple Sara Bernhart

The same chef, August Escoffier, who is responsible for Peach Melba, created this dessert in 1900 for actress Sara Bernhart.

ICE CREAM:
1 pack vanilla ice cream
Zest of one orange
Juice of one orange

SAUCE:
1 1/4 cups pineapple juice
1 tablespoon potato flour

PRESENTATION:
4 rings of pineapple
1/4 cup roasted almonds

Mix ice cream with orange zest and juice, then refreeze. Pour pineapple juice in saucepan, add flour, heat until thickened, cool. Put pineapple rings on a plate, cover with a scoop of ice cream, drizzle sauce over the ice cream and garnish with almonds.

Danish Rum Pudding

W. Clement Stone's favorite. He would come into our Verdandi Club often and loved this dessert.

2 envelopes unflavored gelatin
1/2 cup cold water
6 eggs, separated
1/2 cup sugar
2 cups light cream or milk
3 tablespoons rum or 1/2 teaspoon rum extract
1 cup heavy whipping cream, whipped

Soften gelatin in water. In a large metal bowl, beat egg yolks until lemon colored; gradually add sugar, beat until light and fluffy. Whisk in milk or cream until blended. Place mixture in a double boiler until slightly thickened. Remove from heat and add the gelatin and water mixture. Stir until blended; set bowl over ice water or refrigerate. Stir until thick and syrupy but not set (15-20 minutes); add rum flavoring. Whip egg whites until stiff, fold egg whites and whipped cream into the partially set gelatin, refrigerate until set (overnight). Serve with raspberry sauce (see Peach Melba recipe for sauce.)

Smålands Cheesecake (Ostkaka)

Swedes make this ancient variety of cheesecake in the springtime after the dairy cows have calved. The cows' new milk has rennet in it, which causes the milk to set when heated. I use ricotta cheese or cottage cheese. Either works just fine.

30 ounces of cottage cheese or ricotta (about 3 1/2 cups)
1/2 cup flour
4 eggs
1/4 cup sugar
1/4 cup lemon juice
2 cups heavy cream
1/2 cup finely chopped almonds

Preheat oven to 375 degrees. In a large bowl combine the ricotta, flour, eggs, sugar, lemon juice, and cream. Mix until well blended. Add almonds. Turn into a greased 2-quart baking dish. Place dish in a pan of water and bake for one hour, or until a knife inserted in the center comes out clean. Serve warm or at room temperature with lingonberries or fruit sauce.

Brulé Pudding

1 cup sugar
2 tablespoons hot water

Melt sugar in sauté pan. When melted add water and mix. Pour into an oven-proof dish, making sure the bottom is covered with the sugar mixture.

3 1/4 cups milk
4 eggs
1 tablespoon sugar
1 tablespoon vanilla sugar

Boil milk, pour over beaten eggs. Add sugars. Pour over sugar mixture in the dish. Place in a pan of water and bake for 45-50 minutes at 375 degrees. Let cool, then invert dish onto a serving plate.

Cookies

A Swedish host always serves at least seven types of cookies. Here are some of my favorite recipes.

Basic Butter Cookie

This recipe can be changed by adding various flavorings and by shaping the dough in different ways.

2 sticks butter
1/2 cup sugar
2 1/2 cups sifted all-purpose flour

In a large mixing bowl, combine the ingredients. Use your hands and rub the butter into the flour and sugar. Work the crumbs between the palms of your hands; after a couple of minutes you will have a soft, well-blended dough.

The easiest and quickest way to make uniform-size cookie balls is to divide the dough into four portions, then shape each portion into a long log and cut in twelve. Roll each piece between your palms into a ball and place on a baking sheet.

Bake at 375 degrees for 8 to 10 minutes.

Finnish Sticks (Finska Pinnar)

2 sticks butter
1/3 cup sugar
1 teaspoon almond extract
2 1/2 cups sifted all-purpose flour

GARNISH:
1 beaten egg
Pearl sugar mixed with chopped unblanched almonds

In large mixing bowl, combine the flour, butter, and sugar. Work the dough with your hands until smooth and well-blended. Chill for half an hour.

Preheat oven to 350 degrees. Divide the dough into 6 portions and shape into 16-inch logs. Place the logs parallel with each other and cut into 2-inch pieces. Brush all at once with the beaten egg and sprinkle the garnish of pearl sugar mixed with chopped unblanched almonds over the sticks.

Place cookies on baking sheet and bake for 12 to 15 minutes. Makes 4 dozen.

Ginger Snaps (Pepparkakor)

3 sticks butter (1 1/2 cups)
2 cups sugar
1 cup dark corn syrup
1 1/2 tablespoons ginger
1 1/2 tablespoons cardamom
1 1/2 tablespoons cinnamon
1 tablespoon cloves
1 1/2 cups whipping cream
1 tablespoon baking soda
9 cups sifted all-purpose flour

Cream the butter together with the sugar, syrup, and spices. Add the cream, which has been whipped to a soft foam. Mix the baking soda with half of the flour and add to the batter. Gradually add the remaining flour. Turn the dough onto lightly floured surface and knead until smooth. Return the dough to the bowl, cover, and refrigerate overnight.

Preheat oven to 400 degrees. Roll out part of the dough at a time directly on large baking sheet with nonstick finish. Roll the dough as thin as possible and cut with desired cookie cutters into rounds, hearts, stars, pigs, or other figures. Remove excess dough from the baking sheet. Bake for 5 minutes, or until nicely brown. Set the baking sheet on wire rack; remove the cookies when cool. If desired, decorate the cookies with white frosting:

FROSTING:
2 cups powdered sugar
1 egg white
1 teaspoon white vinegar

Beat together ingredients and fill a pastry tube or paper cone with a fine opening with the frosting and garnish the cookies. Or decorate with blanched almonds before baking. Makes 300 to 400 cookies.

Cinnamon Logs (Kanelkubbar)

Follow the recipe for Finnish Sticks, omitting the teaspoon of almond extract. Garnish with 1/4 cup sugar mixed with 1 teaspoon cinnamon.

Spritz

2 sticks butter
1/2 cup sugar
1 egg yolk
1 teaspoon almond extract
1/3 cup (1 1/2 oz.) blanched almonds
2 1/4 cups sifted all-purpose flour

Preheat oven to 350 degrees. Cream the butter and sugar until light and fluffy. Beat in the egg yolk and almond extract. Grind the almonds and add together with the flour. Work the dough until smooth and well blended. Press it through cookie press into long strips and cut in 4-inch pieces. Shape into rings or Ss and place on baking sheet. Bake for about 10 minutes. Makes 5 dozen.

Chocolate Spritz

1/2 cup powdered sugar
1 tablespoon vanilla sugar
1/3 cup cocoa powder
2 sticks butter
1 egg yolk
2 cups sifted all-purpose flour

In a large mixing bowl, combine the sugar, vanilla sugar, cocoa, butter, and egg yolk. Beat until creamy. Add the flour and work the dough until smooth and well-blended. Chill for half an hour.

Preheat oven to 350 degrees. Press the dough through cookie press into long slender strips, cut them in 4-inch pieces. Shape each piece into a ring and place on baking sheet. Bake for about 10 minutes. When cool top with sifted powdered sugar. Makes 5 dozen.

Dream Cookies (Drömmar) I

2 sticks butter
1 cup sugar
2 teaspoons vanilla sugar
2 1/2 cups sifted all-purpose flour
1/2 teaspoon hjorthornssalt (ammonium carbonate)

Preheat oven to 300 degrees. Cream the butter, sugar, and vanilla sugar until light and fluffy. Add the flour mixed with ammonium carbonate, blend well. Shape the dough into small balls and place on baking sheet. Bake for 20 to 25 minutes. The cookies should be very pale and have a cracked surface. Makes about 5 dozen cookies.

NOTE: Ammonium carbonate is a popular rising agent in Sweden because it gives a special tenderness to rolls and cookies. During baking it will emit a faint odor of ammonia, but this disappears and leaves no trace in the taste of the finished product.

Buy powdered ammonium carbonate at a drugstore or delicatessen.

Dream Cookies (Drömmar) II

These cookies are very delicate and crumble easily, but they are so delicious!

1 stick butter
1 1/4 cups sugar
2 teaspoons vanilla
1/2 cup oil (I use canola oil with extra virgin olive oil)
1 teaspooon ammonium carbonate
2 cups flour
24 almonds (optional)

Cream butter, sugar, and vanilla, Gradually add oil. Mix some of the flour with the ammonium carbonate and stir into creamed mixture. Mix in the remaining flour. Form dough into small balls and place on ungreased baking sheet. Press half an almond on each cookie. Bake at 350 degrees for 15 to 20 minutes. Makes about 4 dozen cookies.

Sand Tarts (Sandbakelser)

1 1/2 sticks butter
1/3 cup sugar
1 egg yolk
1/2 teaspoon almond extract
1/3 cup blanched almonds
1 1/2 cups sifted all-purpose flour

Cream the butter and sugar, beat in the egg yolk and almond extract. Grind the almonds and add together with the flour; mix well. Chill the dough for one hour.

Preheat the oven to 350 degrees. Divide the dough into three portions and shape into long logs. Cut each log in 12 pieces. Use your thumbs and press each piece into a buttered sandbakelse tin. Coat the bottom and the sides with an even layer of the dough.

Place the tins on a baking sheet. Bake for ten to twelve minutes or until light golden. Put the baking sheet on a wire rack and turn the tins upside down. Let cool for 3-4 minutes, then gently tap the bottom of each tin and remove. Makes 3 dozen cookies.

The pastries may be served plain or filled with whipped cream and fruit.

Bread

No list of Swedish recipes would be complete without one for our beloved limpa bread.

Kalix Limpa

Alice from the Land of the Midnight Sun taught me how to make this bread. Kalix is a town in Lappland, not far from where Gösta grew up.

1 lb. brown sugar
2 packages yeast
1/2 teaspoon salt
5 cups lukewarm water
4 eggs
4 lbs. of rye and wheat flour mixed
4 tablespoons fennel
1 tablespoon cardamom (optional)

1/2 cup corn syrup
1/2 cup warm water

Mix sugar, yeast, and salt. Let stand until the sugar melts into yeast, then add lukewarm water. Mix in eggs one at a time, add fennel, and work in flour (reserving enough to use in kneading). Knead until smooth and elastic. Cover and let rise until double in bulk. Bake at 350 degrees. After 15 minutes remove loaves and brush with a mixture of the corn syrup and warm water. Return to oven and bake for 15-20 minutes more and brush again with glaze. Will make 6 round loaves.

You can modify the recipe to your own tastes by adding other spices.

Swedish Cardamom Sweet Bread

This is a wonderful recipe from Bonnie (Bladel) Sparrman, who worked for us at the Sweden Shop for several years. She is now a busy mother and pastor's wife in Shawnee, Kansas. She teaches baking classes to area cooks and is well-known for her cardamom bread and cinnamon rolls.

BASIC DOUGH:

2 (1/4 ounce) packages active dry yeast (4 1/2 teaspoons)
1/4 cup lukewarm water
2 cups milk
1/2 cup unsalted butter, cut into tablespoon-size pieces

1 cup sugar
2 teaspoons salt
2 large eggs, lightly beaten
8 cups all-purpose flour, divided
2 teaspoons ground cardamom

FOR SWEDISH CINNAMON ROLLS:

4 tablespoons unsalted butter, softened
4 tablespoons sugar
4 teaspoons cinnamon
1 large egg white, beaten

FOR ALMOND-FILLED SWEDISH CARDAMOM LOAF:

6 tablespoons almond paste, divided
2 teaspoons cinnamon, divided

FOR CARDAMOM LOAF ICING:

2 tablespoons unsalted butter, softened
1/2 teaspoon almond extract
1/4 cup half-and-half
1 cup confectioners' sugar

TO PREPARE BASIC DOUGH:

Sprinkle yeast over lukewarm water in large mixing bowl and set aside to proof until foamy, about 5 minutes.

Grease a second large mixing bowl and set aside. Line two baking sheets with parchment paper and set aside. Scald the milk in a saucepan until small bubbles form around the perimeter but milk does not boil. Stir the butter, sugar, and salt into the hot milk until well blended. Set aside to cool to lukewarm (about 90 degrees).

When the milk mixture is lukewarm, pour it into the yeast mixture. Add eggs, 4 cups flour, and cardamom; stir until smooth. Stir in 2 to 3 more cups of flour until the dough is solid but still a little sticky. Turn the dough out onto a floured board. Sprinkle dough with more flour. Fold the top half down and knead by pressing the dough all over with the heel of your hand. Turn the dough a quarter turn; sprinkle with more flour and repeat the process. Knead about 5 minutes, or until the dough is elastic and glossy.

Place dough in prepared bowl and cover with greased plastic wrap and a kitchen towel. Allow to rise in a warm (75 to 80 degrees) place until doubled in bulk, about 1 hour.

Gently punch down dough and turn onto a floured surface. With a serrated knife, cut dough in half. Reserve one half for Swedish Cinnamon Rolls. Cut the other half in half; reserve the two portions for Almond-Filled Swedish Cardamom Loaf.

TO MAKE SWEDISH CINNAMON ROLLS:

Roll reserved half of dough into a 12- by 16-inch rectangle on a floured surface. Combine butter, sugar, and cinnamon. Starting at the bottom of the 12-inch side, spread the mixture over the bottom half of the dough. Fold the top half over the bottom half.

Using a pizza wheel or sharp knife, start at the folded edge and cut 12 equal vertical slices. Make a horizontal cut through the middle of the dough so each of the 12 slices is cut in half. Form each piece into a coil and place on a greased baking sheet. Cover with kitchen towels and let rise in a warm place until doubled in bulk, about 45 minutes.

Once the rolls are doubled in bulk, preheat the oven to 365 degrees. Brush each roll with beaten egg white and bake 10 to 12 minues, or until golden brown.

TO MAKE ALMOND-FILLED SWEDISH CARDAMOM LOAF:

Roll each portion of the two reserved dough pieces into a 12- by 16-inch rectangle. Grate half of the almond paste and sprinkle the grated paste and half of the cinnamon over the dough. Roll the dough to make a 16-inch long cylinder. Transfer the cylinder to a greased baking sheet. Using kitchen shears, cut three-fourths way through the dough, every 3/4 inch along both sides of the dough. Turn the slices outward to show the coiled filling and to make a pretty loaf. Repeat the process with the remaining portion of dough. (Two loaves will fit on one baking sheet). Cover with kitchen towels and let rise in a warm place until doubled in bulk, about 45 minutes. Bake at 365 degrees for 18 to 20 minutes, or until golden brown.

After the loaves have cooled, prepare the icing by mixing together all icing ingredients. Drizzle the icing over each loaf.

NOTE: The cinnamon rolls and cardamom loaves can be baked ahead and frozen. Wrap in aluminum foil and store in a large plastic freezer bag. To warm the frozen baked goods, preheat oven to 350 degrees. Place the foil-wrapped rolls or loaves on a baking sheet and warm for about 15 minutes.

Recipe makes 24 cinnamon rolls and 2 cardamom loaves, with 16 servings per loaf.

Var så god!